N WASHINGTON CITY.—[SEE PAGE 278.]

When
the Bells
Tolled for Lincoln

Abraham Lincoln, President of the United States, 1861-1865

When the Bells Tolled for Lincoln

Carolyn L. Harrell

Southern
Reaction to
the Assassination

Mercer University Press
Macon, Georgia

ISBN 0-86554-565-0
ISBN 0-86554-587-1

E457.5
H27
1997

MUP/H423
MUP/P170

Copyright © 1997
Mercer University Press, Macon, Georgia 31210-3960 USA
All rights reserved
Printed in the United States of America

The paper used in this publication meets the minimum requirements of American National Standard for Information Sciences—Permanence of Paper for Printed Library Materials, ANSI Z39.48-1984.

Library of Congress Cataloging-in-Publication Data

Harrell, Carolyn L. (Carolyn Lawton), 1911-
    When the Bells Tolled for Lincoln: Southern Reaction to the
    Assassination /Carolyn L. Harrell
        xiv + 136 pp.   6" x 9" (15 x 22 cm.)
    Includes bibliographical references and index.
    ISBN 0-86554-565-0 (alk. paper)
    ISBN 0-86554-587-1 (alk. paper)
    1. Lincoln, Abraham, 1809-1865—Assassination—Public opinion-
Sources. 2. Public opinion—Southern States—History—19th
century—Sources. 3. United States—History—Civil War, 1861-
1865—Influence—Sources. I. Title.
E457.5.H27 1997
973.7'092—dc21   97-37122
                                                             CIP

Contents

Dedicated to
the memory of MWK

List of Photographs

All photographs are used courtesy of The Lincoln Museum, Fort Wayne, Indiana.

Preface

When bells first tolled the news of Lincoln's death in Washington in the morning hours of 15 April 1865, bells throughout the Union took up the doleful measures. Reactions of disbelief, horror, grief, and anger spread throughout the North. As news of the assassination reached the conquered South, church bells throughout the Confederacy joined in the pealing.

The bells seemed to toll with a united voice, vanquished Confederacy and victorious Union attuned in grief and anguish. But there was discord in the clangor of the bells. On the Good Friday of his murder, Lincoln was, to Northerners, a savior incarnate, a supreme hero, a martyr by whom slaves were freed and a divided nation made whole. In the former Confederacy, however, Southerners blamed Lincoln for their downfall. He became the focus of their hatred, the symbol of their woes. When he died, those who were glad he was gone dared not openly express their elation. They turned, however, to their diaries, letters, and journals where they poured forth their true reactions to the President's assassination.

In his spirited portrait of Lincoln, Stephen B. Oates notes that most new scholarship on Lincoln—touching upon virtually every aspect of his life and appearing in technical monographs and scholarly journal articles—has failed to reach a broad audience.[1]

Indeed, all aspects of Lincoln's life and death, before and during the four years of civil war, including the assassination conspiracy trials, have been explored by historians as well as by lay writers. Some of them, noted Harold M. Hyman, "have since 1885 exploited the Lincoln assassination theme," thereby distressing "present scholarly depictors." According to Hyman the Lincoln literature appearing between 1865 and 1885, almost always written by Northerners, focused on the themes of Confederate guilt and the just verdicts on the Booth group.

---

[1]Stephen B. Oates, *Abraham Lincoln: The Man Behind the Myth* (New York: Harper & Row, 1977), xiv. (Cited hereafter as Oates, *Lincoln*).

In addition the memoirs of secession leaders naturally bore pro-Confederate viewpoint, but largely ignored the assassination.[2]

The handful of secession leaders who did refer to the assassination in their published memoirs were generally reluctant to express any personal opinion regarding the murder of the President. In fact, from the very beginning this studied silence on the part of ex-Confederates seemed to be the rule of day in the defeated South. Whatever the cause, whether fear of reprisal, true indifference, or for reasons they themselves hardly understood, ex-rebels refrained from expressing themselves openly about the assassination.

As news of the assassination spread throughout the defeated Confederacy, terrified rebels tried to suppress their joy, to mask their feelings in silence. Instead, they took up their pens or pencil stubs. They wrote in diaries, letters, journals. They jotted their thoughts in daybooks, scribbled crude drawings in notebooks, and secreted their personal papers from the eyes of the enemy, of whom they spoke only surreptitiously among themselves. As one Georgia planter's wife, Ella Thomas, wrote in her diary: "I shall put my journal in a safe place for I intend to express myself fearlessly and candidly upon all points."[3]

During the Civil War many Confederate government as well as private records were pillaged, burned, scattered, or otherwise obliterated by the invading Union armies. When the capitals of Texas and Louisiana went up in flames, records went with them, as did records in North Carolina where no less than thirty-three county courthouses were reduced to ashes. Countless libraries and trunks and caches of family papers were also lost when the Federals set torch to the dwellings that housed them. In other instances, when Southerners

---

[2]Harold M. Hyman, "With Malice Toward Some: Scholarship (or Something Less) on the Lincoln Murder," Address delivered to the Abraham Lincoln Association, February, 1978. Springfield, Illinois, c. 1979, 20 ff.

[3]Ella Gertrude (Clanton) Thomas Diary, 8 May 1865. Manuscript Department, Duke University Library.

heard the enemy was approaching, rebels themselves burned their private papers to keep them from enemy hands.[4]

Many individual Confederates—those who fled before the enemy, those allowed to remain in their homes in occupied towns and on farms and plantations, as well as paroled rebel soldiers finding their way back home—kept their diaries with them and filled the pages with their inmost thoughts and reactions to events as they occurred. Scores, if not hundreds, of those records now survive in historical collections of Southern universities, in state archives, as well as in smaller, lesser known private, library and archival collections throughout the South. In my search through these collections, I have come upon small leather-bound daybooks for the year 1865, with seams falling apart, the pages yellowed and filled with fading, spidery handwriting. The entries seem to have been made with startling immediacy, at the height of the writer's emotional reaction to events while they were happening. The record is valid, firsthand, and unpremeditated. The frayed papers are the stuff of history, the very essence of historical data.

While I found personal records of a few prominent Confederate military and government officials who wrote in the weeks immediately following the assassination, for the most part I drew from the writings of ordinary citizens of the South: small landowners, tradesmen, prisoners of war, freed slaves, teachers, former plantation and slave owners. There were city officials, rebel soldiers and officers, displaced newspaper editors, clerks, disbarred lawyers, ministers, rabbis, priests and members of their congregations who expressed their reaction to the assassination in their personal writings. Citizens of many Southern towns—Richmond, Savannah, Charleston, Augusta, Macon, Huntsville, Vicksburg, Nashville, Mobile, Charlotte, New Orleans, Baltimore—recorded their views of the assassin's act.

When I began to examine and organize the material in chronological order, according to the locale of the writer—the upper South, the deep South, and the border states—patterns of reaction to Lincoln's

---

[4]Merton Coulter, "What the South Has Done About Its History," *Journal of Southern History*, 2 (February 1936).

assassination became apparent. Each person, each community, each town, each Southern state viewed the assassination in the context of his own concerns and circumstances, as well as within the larger context of a devastated and defeated Confederacy. Reaction differed from person to person, from region to region within a state and from state to state; often from member to member in the same household. Individual reactions were as diverse and personal as the spirits of the people themselves. Overall, a surprising representation of Southern reaction to Lincoln's assassination emerged.

The book is a study of reactions that occurred in the brief period from Lincoln's death until the people in the remotest reaches of the ex-Confederacy absorbed the truth that Lincoln had been felled by an assassin's bullet. In undertaking to assess immediate responses to the murder, many questions arise. Why did Southerners react to the event as they did? How did they express their feelings? Why were some gleeful? What are we to make of the mute, seemingly indifferent reactions of others? What can we learn from a comparison of reactions from the upper South, the deep South, the border states? What were their reactions when the slain president was laid to rest and the country's leadership passed into the hands of Andrew Johnson?

Valid answers to such questions require an understanding of the milieu of the Confederate South. Throughout the early national period the Southern states deceveloped a kinship for each other based on their agricultural economy and the firm conviction of the legitimacy of the Southern way of life based on low-skilled slave labor. When the "Black Republican" Lincoln was elected President, they cemented their already strong bond by seceding from the Union and creating the Confederate States of America. In so doing, the Southern states made civil war a reality by forming a united front to protect their lives and property against the "diabolical" new president and his "nefarious" and belligerent policies.

When Lincoln was assassinated at the beginning of his second term, Southerners' fears were compounded by alarm over what might now become of them. Upon hearing of the murder, the former rebels, now living under the rule of Union armies, responded almost immediately with a gamut of emotions—elation, depair, mute indifference—depending on their personal beliefs and circumstances. These emotions had hardly subsided when they experienced new concerns and fears that their beloved South would fare even worse under the "scalawag" president Andrew Johnson.

They almost universally felt that their fate would have been kinder had Lincoln lived to guide the nation's affairs. They came to regret Lincoln's demise and to resent him less. Eventually, they came to appreciate his efforts to achieve, as he said in his Second Inaugural, "a just and lasting peace among ourselves and with all nations."

Some mysteries about Abraham Lincoln *and* about the American South may never be solved. One thing, however, is certain: Although Southerners' tenacious and proud love of their region was not shaken, they nonetheless eventually came to regard Lincoln with respect and admiration, if not love.

I owe much to those who have advised and assisted me in preparing this study. Above all, I am indebted to Professor Gerald S. Henig, California State University, Hayward, who suggested the subject, and who advised and encouraged me with constructive criticism throughout the entire process of researching, developing, and writing the book. When I was considering writing on the subject, Professors Hans L. Trefousse, Richard N. Current, and Stephen B. Oates, as well as Mark E. Neely, Jr., Director of the Louis A. Warren Lincoln Library and Museum, encouraged me to proceed with the project, pointing out that Southern reaction to Lincoln's assassination was a badly misunderstood subject and that there was no booklength study on the matter. I am also indebted to Professor Harold M. Hyman of Rice University, who at the book's inception helped me to define a realistic goal.

During my visits to various universities and libraries for research in their collections, the directors and their staffs were invariably gracious and generous with their time and talents in making available their materials. Caroline Wire, Assistant to the Director of Libraries, Louisiana State University, was helpful far beyond the call of duty, as were Robert Martin and Stone Miller of the university's special collections libraries. Charles Royster, Professor of History, and Waldo W. Braden, Professor Emeritus of Speech, Louisiana State University, shared with me their knowledge of Lincoln and his relationship with the Confederate South. Mattie Russell, Director Emeritus, Ellen Gartrell, and Robert Byrd advised and assisted me in the Manuscript and Special Collections of Duke University; and Professor Robert F. Durden at Duke shared his knowledge of available source material. At the University of North Carolina, my appreciation and thanks go to Richard Shrader, Director, and to the staff of the Southern Historical Collection. My appreciation and thanks go also to Nancy Parker of the Woodson Research Center, Rice University, and to Richard E. Lindemann, Reference Archivist, Emory University.

James Gilreath, American history specialist, and James H. Hutson, Chief, Manuscript Division of the Library of Congress, made available materials and microfilm that were especially significant to the study, as did Randy Roberts, Manuscript Specialist for the collections at the University of Missouri. At the Georgia Department of Archives and History, I am indebted to Virginia Shadron, Research Consultant and Richard Couch, Archivist.

For specific help in numerous areas and countless ways, I am indebted to Margaret Henson, Anne White Fuller, René Pruitt, Ellen Flaharty and David Lilly and their associates in the Heritage Room, Interlibrary Loan, and Reference Department of the Huntsville, Alabama, Public Library. I want especially to thank Helen Crutchfield Johnson, who twice read the manuscript with care and furnished a thoughtful and detailed critique, and my daughters and their husbands: Mary and Charles Reeves and Lyn and Jim Foley. They have all been supportive and helpful in numerous ways, as has my grandson-in-law, Craig Duncan. With much gratitude I single out Andrew Manis, my editor at Mercer University Press. His astute and insightful editing enhanced the book immeasurably.

Carolyn L. Harrell
Houston, Texas

Introduction:
The Vanquished South

Lee surrendered on 9 April 1865. At Appomattox Courthouse in Virginia, the general signed the letter of surrender, rose from his chair, and extended his hand to Grant. As he left, he stood in the doorway for a moment, gazing into the distance. A crimson flush rose from his neck and spread over his face. He squared his shoulders and stepped into the courtyard, mounted Traveler, and reined him onto the road to the rebel encampment. When Lee's men saw him approaching, they raised their battered hats to cheer him as always, but something in his demeanor gave them pause. As he entered their lines, they lowered their hats and crowded around the horse, their gaunt, sleepless faces upturned. "Men," he said, "I have done for you all that it was in my power to do. You have done your duty. Leave the result to God. Go to your homes and resume your occupations. Obey the laws and become as good citizens as you were soldiers." Tears welled in his eyes. After a pause, he murmured, "Goodbye."[1]

The capitol was blasted awake in the early morning hours when word of Lee's surrender arrived in Washington. A deafening salute of five hundred guns brought the people swarming into the street around the White House, cheering, dancing, waving flags, mad with joy. Lincoln came to his window and looked down upon the surging crowd. The jubilation became almost uncontrollable. As the tall, thin figure stood silently there, the crowd became quiet, looking toward their President, expecting a speech. He congratulated the people in "this hour of triumph," but spoke only briefly, saying he would speak publicly the following evening, at which time he would address the critical issues that were facing the nation as a result of Lee's surrender. During the hours until Lincoln made the promised speech, he contem-

---

[1]Charles Bracelen Flood, *Lee: The Last Years* (Boston: Houghton-Mifflin, 1981), 11-13, 15; E. B. Long, *The Civil War Day by Day* (Garden City, New York: Doubleday and Company, 1971), 671.

plated the great problem: putting the seceded states back into "proper practical relation" with the Union, and binding together again, in spirit and in truth, the United States of America.[2] It would be no easy task.

The Confederacy was utterly defeated; the very foundations of the Southern world had been destroyed. Already before Lee had signed the document of surrender, many Southern cities had fallen into enemy hands. Some had been reduced to ashes, their citizens had fled or were cringing in the shells of their houses, their lives and livelihood under the control of the occupying armies. Throughout the South lands that year after year had produced crops of "white gold" now lay blackened and fallow. Those who tilled the lands as slaves were now free. A quarter million of the South's sons were dead, some imprisoned, others in exile. From the big plantation houses surrounded by their coveys of cabins and their now destroyed fields, to the twisted railroad tracks, to the piles of cotton bales smouldering on the wharves, to the smallest village cottages nestled among the pewless churches and gutted small-town stores--all had been demolished. So profound was the damage that more than a hundred years later the wounds had not completely healed. And many a Southerner laid the responsibility for the atrocities of the war, for the war itself, at the feet of President Abraham Lincoln. Hatreds converged on him with an intensity so great that many could scarcely speak his name without reddening. Politically, the nation was reunited at Appomattox. It would be decades before spiritual reunion became a reality.

Throughout the Union, news of General Grant's victory over Lee produced unabashed rejoicing; throughout the South, however, there was lamentation and deep sorrow. But there was also a measure of relief that the fighting was over. Surely the worst was behind them. Both the conquered and the conquerors turned to God in prayer. A Northern minister gave thanks for the "great leader of our armies whom [H]e has used as [H]is instrument to save the nation." Southerners prayed "to an

---

[2]Roy P. Basler, *The Collected Works of Abraham Lincoln,* vol. 8 (New Brunswick, NJ: Princeton University Press, 1953), 403.

all-wise God" for mercy, for bread, for "our fallen leaders," for returning sons, and for delivery from "the enemy in our midst."[3]

Whatever the future might hold for ex-rebels, one thing was certain: the past four years of war, in terms of lives lost and property destroyed, were unprecedented. Indeed no Union general epitomized the destructiveness of the conflict better than did William Tecumseh Sherman. In September 1864 General Sherman had sat on his horse on a hill overlooking Atlanta. He turned to look upon the scene of his latest battle, the city smoldering and in ruins. The black smoke rose high in the air and hung like a pall over the area. Later he recorded the event: "The day was extremely beautiful . . . and an unusual feeling of exhilaration seemed to pervade all minds . . . ." After he left Atlanta, at the end of his sweep through Georgia, Sherman had made President Lincoln a Christmas gift: the city of Savannah. He then turned his efforts toward South Carolina, which was "where treason began," and "where," he swore, "it will end."[4]

Emma LeConte, whose professor father had been called from his teaching post at South Carolina College in Columbia to serve as a consulting chemist to the Confederate States' Nitre and Mining Bureau, could "breathe more freely now, but not less sadly." The destruction and desolation that had surrounded Emma in Columbia had little impact on her, given the overriding fear that the city itself might be invaded. Now that Lee had surrendered, she could focus more clearly on the damage inflicted upon her community:

> There is not a house in Columbia, I believe, that has not been pillaged. Those that the flames spared were entered by brutal soldiers and everything wantonly destroyed. . . .

---

[3]*New York Times,* 10 April 1865, 4; Bryan/Willingham/Lawton Papers, Letter dated 24 May 1865, Albany, Georgia, Annie Willingham to "Asbury," Georgia State Archives, Atlanta, Georgia.

[4]Mills B. Lane, ed. *William T. Sherman* (Savannah, GA: The Beehive Press, 1974), 147-148; Carl Sandburg, *Storm Over the Land: A Profile of the Civil War* (New York: Harcourt Brace, 1939), 361ff.

As far as the eye could see, only spectre-like chimneys and the shattered walls, all flooded over by the rich moonlight which gave them a mysterious but mellow softness and quite took from them the ghastly air which they wear in the sunlight. . . . At the market place we saw the old bell . . . that had rung out every state as it seceded, lying half buried in the earth and reminding me of Retzach's last line in "The song of the Bell," showing that "all things earthly disappear."[5]

Before Lee signed the surrender papers at Appomattox, Petersburg and Richmond both had fallen. Confederate President Jefferson Davis and his cabinet had left Richmond during the night of April 2, 1865, making up a trainload of fleeing officials and their families. John B. Jones, a clerk in the office of the Secretary of War, noted in his day book, "[T]he government [has] gone." He added ruefully, "There was no provision for civil employees and their families."[6]

With son Tad in hand, Lincoln visited Richmond "to have a look" at the rebel capital that had surrendered only hours before. (See photo, facing page.) With smoke still floating overhead, exultant blacks still dancing in the streets, and citizens of Richmond peering from behind shuttered windows, Lincoln walked toward the Capitol, led by a detachment of Union cavalry. In the Capitol building he rested, then spent a short time sauntering through the structure.[7]

---

[5]Emma LeConte Diary, 14 April 1865; 17 May 1865, LeConte Papers, Southern Historical Collection, University of North Carolina, Chapel Hill; Earl Schenck, Miers, ed. *When the World Ended: The Diary of Emma LeConte* (New York: Oxford University Press, 1957), x-xi, 14, 57, 85, 87, 99.

[6]John B. Jones, *A Rebel War Clerk's Diary*, Earl Schenck Miers, ed. (New York: A. S. Barnes, 1961), ix-xi, 533-538. Diary entries for April 1865. Jones served as Clerk under each of five secretaries of war, each of whom claimed importance as a statesman of the Lost Cause. Jones is said to have written his diary with President Jefferson Davis' knowledge and approval. He is reported to have said that his function in the government until the end of its career was "very important," and his "discretionary friends will understand why I accepted the poor title of clerkship. . . ."

[7]Virginius Dabney. *Richmond, the Story of a City* (Garden City, NY: Doubleday, 1976), 194.

Lincoln and his son Tad entering Richmond after the city's surrender to Union forces, 3 April 1865. (The Lincoln Museum, Fort Wayne, Indiana, No. 4337)

When Judith McGuire heard of Lincoln's visit to the former Confederate Capitol, she complained:

Ah, It is a bitter pill. I would that dear old house, with all its associations, so sacred to Southerners, so sweet to us as a family, had shared in the general conflagration. Then its history would have been unsullied, though sad. Oh, how gladly would I have seen it burn![8]

The *New Orleans Tribune*, which the rebels called, "the enemy's press among us," blazoned the headlines: "GLORIOUS NEWS: LEE SURRENDERS," and printed an order from the Provost Marshal to celebrate the victory.[9] New Orleans, the first city to come under Federal control, was under martial law, and, according to some observers, the conquerors, by arrest, confiscation, and persecution, were trying to break the morale of the "city which never surrendered."[10] In a spirit of "thanking their stars they were all as well off as they were," the citizens gathered on Lafayette Square to eulogize President Lincoln and General Grant, with cannon salutes, band playing, and flag waving of the Stars and Stripes. They had no choice.[11]

The news of Lee's surrender trickled into Florida, circulated largely by word of mouth. The raising of the Stars and Stripes over the state Capitol in Tallahassee, accompanied by little trauma and little fanfare, marked the end of Confederate Florida.[12] Augusta, Georgia, was left unconquered by the enemy's armies, but it had become demoralized and overrun by rogues who robbed the government stores and harassed

---

[8]Judith Brockenbrough McGuire, *Diary of a Southern Refugee* (New York: Doubleday, 1968), 350.

[9]*New Orleans Tribune*, 15 April 1865.

[10]Dabney, *Richmond*, 175, 185; *New Orleans Daily Picayune*, 13 and 26 April 1862.

[11]Mark E. Neely, Jr., *The Abraham Lincoln Encyclopedia* (New York: McGraw-Hill, 1982), 42, 259, 331.

[12]John E. Johns, *Florida During the Civil War*. (Gainesville, FL: University of Florida Press, 1963), 206.

the people to such a degree that nothing was safe. Near the end of the war, Augusta came to be known as the Eldorado of sutlers, cotton thieves, speculators, and "other such riffraff." In the midst of this discord, confusion, and lawlessness, preludes of peace became music to the ears of Augustans, and news of Appomattox caused hardly a stir.[13]

Perhaps Eva Jones best characterized what Lee's defeated and disbanded army would find when they finally arrived at home. In the closing days of the war, she fled to Augusta as the enemy approached the family plantation at Montevideo. Now residing with relatives and friends, she wrote:

> We have seen hope after hope fall blighted and withering about us, until our country is no more—merely a heap of ruins and ashes. A joyless future of probable ignominy, poverty, and want is all that spreads before us. . . . You see, it is with no resigned spirit that I yield to the iron yoke our conqueror forges for his fallen and powerless foe.[14]

Lee surrendered on Palm Sunday; the following Good Friday Lincoln was felled by an assassin's bullet. What was the reaction, or more precisely, what were the reactions, of Southerners to the murder of the leader whose "depraved human heart" in the view of Eva Jones brought "sorrow" and "unmerited punishment" to so many? What contributed to such strong emotions; such joy over the death of a president who professed only the highest motives in saving the Union? Why did they not dare express such joy openly? How was it that a people could fix their enmity so tenaciously on one man?

---

[13]Florence Fleming Corley, *Confederate City: Augusta, Georgia.* (Columbia: University of South Carolina Press, 1960), 93.

[14]Robert Manson Myers, ed., *The Children of Pride* (New Haven: Yale University Press, 1972), 1273-1275. Myers's book is composed of Jones family correspondence, arranged in chronological order, without emendation, and without editorial comment. The quotations throughout this book are from the letters as they appear on the cited pages of Myers's book. See "A Note on Sources."

On the other hand, why was it that some in the South expressed equally profound emotions of loss and mourning at the death of the enemy's President? Where did the bells toll in true mourning? Why in some places was there a mixture of joy and grief in the ringing bells? How, indeed, did this man, variously described as "Honest Abe" or the "Devil incarnate," appear to Southerners whom Lincoln described in no harsher terms than "my erring brethren" and "my dissatisfied fellow-countrymen?"[15]

---

[15]*Alexandria (Virginia) Gazette*, as quoted, 20 March 1865; Davis, *Image of Lincoln*, 36.

Chapter 1

The South's Lincoln

B efore 1860 the South knew Lincoln hardly at all. Until then, Lincoln was a relative unknown, his political actions unnoticed in the South. Lincoln had served in the Illinois State Legislature and later for a single term as the lone Whig representative from Illinois in the United States Congress. After the Whig party disintegrated, Lincoln joined the Republican Party, steadfastly determined to become the leader of his state and section. In a series of debates with Stephen A. Douglas, he vied for Douglas' seat in the Senate. Addressing the great issue of those debates, Lincoln again and again insisted that slavery must be excluded from the territories. He declared in 1858, "A house divided against itself cannot stand, I believe the government cannot endure permanently half slave and half free."[1]

Convinced that the very future of the country was at stake, he believed the territories must be kept free; slavery should not extend beyond the states where it already existed. Lincoln lost the senate contest to Douglas, but he made many Republican friends in the course of the campaign. These friends quickly began to mention him as a dark horse candidate for president, and in May 1860 they nominated him at the Republican National Convention in Chicago. On the third ballot, Lincoln became the party's standard bearer.

The South now began to take notice of him. What little they learned of the "Black Republican," as they called him, they did not like. Lincoln and his running mate, Hannibal Hamlin, were so little known

---

[1]Don E. Fehrenbacher, *Prelude to Greatness: Lincoln in the 1850's* (Stanford, California: Stanford University Press, 1962). See the chapter on Lincoln's speech at the Illinois Republican State Convention; Allan Nevins, *The Emergence of Lincoln: Douglas, Buchanan, and Party Chaos 1857-1859*, vol. 1 (New York: Charles Scribner's Sons, 1950), 7-8, 359.

that the *New Orleans Picayune* complained, "[T]he political biographers have not thought it proper to send us [in] advance [an] extended memoir of their lives in aid of the journalists." Not having verifiable biographical information about Lincoln, many Southern editors took to composing editorials and stories from whatever hearsay sources and word-of-mouth tidbits they could scrape together. The *San Antonio Ledger and Texan* called Lincoln "a bold, vulgar, unscrupulous abolitionist, without any experience in administrative affairs." The *Macon Daily Telegraph* called him a "strong and rough candidate." Although it was probably true that *any* Republican nominee would have yielded the same response in the South that Lincoln's nomination did, the North Carolina *Wilmington Daily Journal* put it succinctly: "Lincoln embodies a system with an avowed object, that object being the ultimate extermination of slavery."[2]

The *Charleston Mercury* stated flatly, "at the next Presidential election, the question is not . . . a Democratic or Black Republican President, but union or disunion." A fiery editorial in the *Atlanta Southern Confederacy* pronounced, "[T]he loyal South, the Constitutional South, will never submit to such humiliation and degradation as an inauguration of Abraham Lincoln."[3] The Southern press became almost unanimous in its disapproval of Lincoln. For the most part they became too involved in Southern campaign battles, in which Lincoln figured only as a bogeyman to be resisted, not as a serious politician to be defeated. Voters in the South recoiled from the "Black Republican." The South's votes were sectional in nature, with lively contests among Democratic candidates John C. Breckinridge and Stephen A. Douglas. Breckinridge eventually became Lincoln's opponent in the 1860 election with a platform to "protect the rights of persons and property

---

[2]*New Orleans Picayune*, 9 June 1860; *San Antonio Ledger and Texan*, May 26, 1860; *Macon (Georgia) Daily Telegraph*, May 29, 1860; *Wilmington (North Carolina) Daily Journal*, May 24, 1860.

[3]*Charleston Mercury*, 16 April 1860, quoted in Michael Davis, *The Image of Lincoln in the South* (Knoxville: The University of Tennessee Press, 1971, 11; *Atlanta Southern Confederacy*, quoted by *New York Times*, 7 August 1860.

in the Territories and wherever else its Constitutional authority extended."[4]

Before the Civil War, the basic elements of the economic life of the South were relatively simple: fertile soil, a mild climate, and low-skilled laborers of African-descent to till the soil. Above all, its economy was based on slavery. The "peculiar institution," as Southerners called it, was most vital in the deep South, consisting of South Carolina, Georgia, Alabama, Mississippi, Louisiana, Texas, and Florida. There the proportion of slaves-to-masters, of blacks-to-whites, was largest, and where the advocates of state sovereignty were most vocal. In the upper South—North Carolina, Tennessee, Arkansas, and Virginia—slavery was relatively less important economically, and the ratio of blacks-to-whites was much smaller. The border states—Delaware, Maryland, Kentucky and Missouri—had the smallest black population of all, consisting of slaves and a large number of free blacks. There were free blacks in the North, of course, but the economy was not dependent on their labors. The North's economic life was punctuated by rapidly developing technology and labor-saving machinery.[5]

At the time Lincoln received the nomination, the divisions in the North and South had become real, wide, and very deep. In both North and South, distrust, anger, and alarm were rampant. The tensions between the sections were rife with unresolved differences: to the South, slavery was right, a positive good; to the North, slavery was wrong, a positive evil. In the North, maintaining the Union intact and the non-extension of slavery were of prime importance; in the South, maintaining slavery was paramount, even it if meant secession from the Union.

---

[4]Donald E. Reynolds, *Editors Make War: Southern Newspapers in the Secession Crisis* (Nashville, Tennessee: Vanderbilt University Press, 1970), 94; Kenneth C. Davis, *Don't Know Much About the Civil War* (New York: William Morrow and Company, 1996).

[5]Harold M. Hyman and William M. Wiecek, *Equal Justice Under Law, Constitutional Development, 1835-1875* (New York: Harper & Row, Publishers, 1982), 204; Harold M. Hyman, *Era of the Oath: Northern Loyalty Tests During the Civil War and Reconstruction* (Philadelphia: University of Pennsylvania Press, 1959), ii.

Differing ideological convictions were not divided rigidly along state lines: some upheld the Southern cause in the North and there were Union supporters in the South. As the country moved inevitably toward war in the months between the Republican Convention and the inauguration of the new President, the division of families in the border states became especially poignant and hurtful. And there were those in the South who had grave misgivings about the "rightness" of slavery.[6]

Southern newspapers, often the sole disseminator of news through-out the South, were almost all narrowly political in their emphasis. A few Southern readers subscribed to Northern publications of general interest, but the number of literate, well-informed, "reading" citizens was relatively small. Southerners got the regional and political "facts" from Southern newspapers.

Southern Democratic sheets endorsed a wide variety of favorites for President: Jefferson Davis, Andrew Johnson, John C. Breckinridge, Stephen A. Douglas and others. Like the editor of the *Atlanta Daily Intelligencer,* some thought that it mattered little which Democratic nominee reached the White House, so long as he was firmly committed to a "sound platform, such as every *true* Democrat North and South can consistently stand upon." What really mattered to Southerners was that a Republican be kept out of the White House. They were convinced that a Republican President would mean the ultimate abolition of slavery. In fact, any Northern candidate seemed to pose a threat. A number of newspapers opposed Douglas as a *Northern* Democrat.[7]

Southern editors were engrossed in a bitter political war among themselves in the summer of 1860. Most focused their energies on the two Democratic contenders—Douglas, the Northern Democratic candidate, and Breckinridge, the Southern Democratic candidate. They paid little attention to the Republican platform, and even less to the

---

[6]Stephen B. Oates, *With Malice Toward None: The Life of Abraham Lincoln* (New York: Harper & Row, 1977), New American Library Edition, 38-39, 42, 115-116; Mark E. Neely, Jr., *The Abraham Lincoln Encyclopedia* (New York: McGraw-Hill, 1982), 217-218.

[7]Reynolds, *Editors Make War,* 4-7, 32, 94.

candidate. In fact, Lincoln's name rarely appeared in Southern newspapers during the first few months of the campaign. The pro-Breckinridge *Atlanta Daily Intelligencer* explained that "since Mr. Lincoln [has] no party in our State, we have not thought it proper to spend much of our ammunition upon him."[8]

Audley Smith, a Georgian visiting in New York shortly after Lincoln's nomination, wrote to his uncle in South Georgia:

> Political parties are comparatively quiet [in New York]. The Republican candidates the only ones nominated as yet. Here and there you will see in full the names of Lincoln and Hamlin, but the chances of their election are not brilliant. . . The whole national heart seems to beat through this organ [New York] of our republic, and disunion is impossible. Our reason leaves us the day we agree to dissolve so sacred and essential a tie and bond. The South had her *friends* as well as her foes in the Northern States; and could the subject subside politically, peace and harmony would be restored.[9]

That possibility did not seem likely. From the very beginning of the campaign, most Southerners were clearly prejudiced toward Lincoln. Lincoln did little to clarify his position for his dissatisfied fellow-countrymen in the South.[10] After his nomination, he became a reluctant speaker, fearing that whatever he said might be misconstrued. After all, his position on slavery extension was well-known. Any further elaboration might do more harm than good. As a result, he refused to speak, asking, "Kindly let me be silent." Southern Unionists and Northern friends of the South alike urged Lincoln to issue an authoritative statement to allay anxiety, to compose the public mind. William S. Speer of Shelbyville, Tennessee, persisted in asking Lincoln to disclaim all intention to interfere with slavery in the States. Lincoln's curt answer

---

[8]*Atlanta Daily Intelligencer*, 31 March 1860.
[9]Myers, *Children of Pride*, 353-354.
[10]Neely, *Lincoln Encyclopedia*, x, 353-354.

was "[It] will do no good. I have already done this many times; and it is in print, and open to all who will read. . . . If they hear not the prophets, neither will they be persuaded though one rose from the dead." Whenever he did speak publicly in the summer of 1860, he kept his speeches short and his remarks general. What his opponents could understand of Lincoln they abhorred; what they could not understand of him, they feared.[11]

It was no surprise, therefore, that news of Lincoln's election precipitated immediate reaction in the South. On 20 December 1860, South Carolina was the first Southern state to secede. Six other slave states, all from the deep South, followed within a month and a half. When delegates from the seceding states met in Montgomery, Alabama, on 4 February 1861, they adopted a constitution, and elected Jefferson Davis President and Alexander H. Stephens Vice-President of the new Confederate States of America.[12]

While jubilant over events in Montgomery, the *New Orleans Daily Delta* burst into a scathing and villifying evaluation of Lincoln as he made the trip from his home in Illinois to Washington to assume his duties as president:

He never opens his mouth but he puts his foot into it. In supreme silliness—in profound ignorance of the institutions of the Republic of which he had been chosen chief—in dishonest and cowardly efforts to dodge responsibility and play a double part—in disgusting levity on the most serious subjects, the speeches of Lincoln on his way to the capital have no equals in the history of any people, civilized or semi-civilized.[13]

---

[11]Waldo W. Braden, "Kindly Let Me Be Silent: A Reluctant Lincoln," *Lincoln Herald* 86 (Winter 1984) 4: 194-201; Richard N. Current, *The Lincoln Nobody Knows* (New York: Hill and Wang, 1963), 84.

[12]Harold M. Hyman, *Union and Confidence, The 1860s* (New York: Thomas Y. Crowell, 1976), 47.

[13]*New Orleans Daily Delta*, 26 February 1861.

Savannah's Mayor Charles Colcock Jones, Jr. expressed a similar opinion: "Mr. Lincoln's inaugural may foreshadow something of the Black Republican policy. His speeches in advancing to Washington were certainly ridiculous." He added ominously, "Our large guns are not here as yet. They are, however, daily expected."[14]

Lincoln worked on his inaugural address for more than a month, assisted by trusted advisors who carefully reviewed it. He was now ready to speak, to answer questions that had been pressed upon him, to state his policy. On 4 March 1861, after taking the oath of office, he delivered his inaugural address while standing on the steps of the Capitol.

> I have no purpose, directly or indirectly, to interfere with the institution of slavery in the states where it exists. I believe I have no right to do so. I now reiterate these sentiments . . . and in doing so I only press upon the public attention the most conclusive evidence of which the case is susceptible that the property, peace and security of no section are to be in any wise endangered by the now incoming administration.
>
> [N]o State upon its own mere motion can lawfully get out of the Union . . . . [R]esolves and ordinances to that effect are legally void . . . . [A]cts of violence within any State or States against the authority of the United States are insurrectionary or revolutionary. . . . I therefore consider that in view of the Constitution and the laws, the Union is unbroken and . . . I shall take care, as the Constitution itself expressly enjoins upon me, that the laws of the Union be faithfully executed in all the States. . . . I trust this will not be regarded as a menace, but only as the declared purpose of the Union that *will* constitutionally defend and maintain itself. . .
>
> In doing this there needs to be no bloodshed or violence, and there shall be none unless it be forced upon the national

---

[14]Letter of Charles C. Jones Jr. to his father, 5 March 1861, quoted in Myers, *Children of Pride*, 655.

authority. . . . In *your* hands, my dissatisfied fellow-countrymen, and not in *mine*, is the momentous issue of civil war. . . . We are not enemies, but friends. We must not be enemies. Though passion may have strained it must not break our bonds of affection.[15]

While border state conservatives found reason for hope of peace and reunion in his words, many Confederates scorned the address as ambiguous and threatening. To Emma Holmes his speech was just what was expected of him, "stupid, ambiguous, vulgar, and insolent, and everywhere considered a virtual declaration of war."[16]

The Southern press took an exceedingly dim view of his speech. The *Nashville Union and American* called the address, "a declaration of war against the seceded States," as did the editor of the *Richmond Dispatch*, who proclaimed, "The inaugural address . . . inaugurates Civil War." The *New Orleans Delta* put it a bit more mildly, "We are compelled to regard [Lincoln's inaugural address] as a very inferior production, whether considered as a literary, logical, or statesmanlike production. . . [It] is involved and inconclusive."[17]

On the day of the inauguration, Edmund Ruffin, former editor of the *Farmer's Register* and an avid promoter of Southern independence, read the words of Lincoln's inaugural address as they were posted at the telegraph office in Charleston. For Ruffin, Lincoln's speech settled the question. "There must be war," he wrote in his diary that very day, and with a mixture of excitement, impatience, and glee, he followed Lincoln's actions from then on as he awaited developments in the Union and in the Confederacy.[18]

---

[15]Roy P. Basler, ed. *The Collected Works of Abraham Lincoln* (New Brunswick, New Jersey: Rutgers University Press, 1953-1955, 9 vols.), 4:426.

[16]Davis, *Image*, 36; Page Smith, *Trial by Fire: A People's History of the Civil War* (New York: McGraw Hill, 1982), 30.

[17]*Nashville Union and American*, 5 March 1861: *Richmond Dispatch*, 5 March 1861.

[18]Betty L. Mitchell, *Edmund Ruffin: A Biography* (Bloomingdale: Indiana University Press, 1981), 174-75.

As late as 10 April, however, more than a month after the inauguration, Mayor Jones and his fellow Savannahians were still unable to come to grips with Lincoln's position. In anticipation of "hostile demonstrations," as the Mayor expressed it, the citizens became busily engaged in getting their defenses in order.[19]

Fort Sumter was the only facility remaining under Federal authority in Charleston Harbor. Without bloodshed, South Carolina had seized Fort Moultrie and other Federal holdings in the area. Now at Fort Sumter, Major Robert J. Anderson, in charge of the garrison stationed there, was hanging on in the face of ever diminishing supplies of food and provisions for his troops. On Saturday, 7 April, Charleston authorities cut off all supplies and communications to Fort Sumter, and the following day President Lincoln sent a notice to South Carolina Governor F. W. Pickens advising him that a naval expedition would be sent to provision the beleaguered garrison. Nobody really knows what was in Lincoln's mind when he decided to send the provisions to Sumter. Some say he followed a strategy of defense; others insist that it was a declaration of war. The *Daily Express* of Petersburg, Virginia, declared, "He chose to draw the sword." Whatever Lincoln's intent, the first gun was indeed fired by a Confederate. When General P. G. T. Beauregard received word that relief was on the way for Anderson, he promptly gave orders to fire the first gun that formally began the Civil War. Ruffin was exultant. His fellow Palmetto Guard Volunteers unanimously agreed that the honor of firing the first shot at Sumter should go to their oldest recruit, Edmund Ruffin. When the signal came in the early hours of Friday morning, Ruffin was ready by his loaded cannon. By noon on Saturday, a waving white flag announced Anderson's surrender. Quietly, with the Stars and Stripes lowered and folded away, the major took the flag and marched his garrison from Sumter.[20]

The people of Charleston were jubilant. Young Mary Chesnut did not even pretend to sleep that night. Neither could anyone else in

---

[19]Myers, *Children of Pride*, 663.
[20]Mitchell, *Ruffin*, 175-77: Current, *Lincoln Nobody Knows*, 118.

Charleston. At 4:00 a.m., the sound of pealing bells reached her ears, followed by the noise of roaring cannon. To her the bells of St. Michael's church seemed to ring interminably. In Columbia, South Carolina, later that same morning, the church bells began to toll in unison. To thirteen-year-old Emma LeConte at her home near the campus of South Carolina College, the whole town seemed in joyful tumult. In Richmond, bonfires blazed in front of the offices of the city's three newspapers, the *Enquirer*, the *Examiner*, and the *Dispatch*. Only the office of the *Richmond Whig*, a Unionist newspaper, remained dark.[21]

As far as most Confederates were concerned, Lincoln bore the responsibility for starting the war. The editor of a North Carolina newspaper, heretofore staunchly Unionist, declared, "It is a war which could not have been avoided. It has been forced upon us! We must fight!"[22]

Jefferson Davis was ready to take Sumter by force even before he heard that Lincoln was sending a relief expedition to Anderson at the fort. Lincoln, with "solemn resignation" announced to his assembled cabinet on April 13 that the rebels had fired the first shot, forcing him to make a decision of "immediate dissolution or blood." President Davis, equally vehement, announced to the Confederate Congress that the responsibility for launching the war was Lincoln's. "[T]he South will *meet* not wage the war—war now launched by Lincoln," Davis declared. And he repeated as he had many times before, "All we ask is to be let alone."[23]

Two days after the fall of Sumter, Lincoln sent the states a proclamation calling for 75,000 militiamen. Now vacillators both North and South, as well as Southern state governments on the verge

---

[21]Mary Boykin Chesnut, *A Diary from Dixie* (New York: Peter Smith, 1919), Entry for 12 April 1861; Earl Schenck Miers, ed., *Emma LeConte*, x: *Memphis Appeal*, 18 April 1861.

[22]Reynolds, *Editors Make War*, 203-204.

[23]Neely, *Lincoln Encyclopedia*, 285; Shelby Foote, *The Civil War: A Narrative* (New York: Random House, 1963), 55.

of secession, were forced to take sides and declare allegiance either to the Union or to the Confederacy.[24]

In the view of most Southerners, Lincoln's actions, especially his call for 75,000 troops, represented concrete evidence of his utter deceitfulness. Had he not declared there would be no invasion, no use of force against, or among the people anywhere? Lincoln was the instigator; he initiated the conflict. Their bitterness toward him grew apace.

By the time of the attack on Fort Sumter, the seven seceded states had operated as the Confederate States of America for two months. The eight remaining Southern states had clung tenaciously to the Union, while border statesmen attempted to construct a compromise. Lincoln's call for a militia ended all talk of compromise. In the upper South secession conventions began to spring into action. On 17 April, the Virginia convention adopted an ordinance of secession that was soon ratified. Once the Old Dominion joined the Confederacy, the secessionists moved their capital from Montgomery to Richmond. Promptly Arkansas, North Carolina, and Tennessee joined the Confederacy, but border states Delaware, Maryland, Missouri, and Kentucky, were unwilling to become the battleground for the impending conflict and remained loyal.[25]

Closely following these events, Savannah's Mayor Jones was pleased to hear that the Virginia legislators passed an ordinance of secession, and that North Carolinians were realizing the importance of decided action. He was especially gratified at Kentucky Governor Beriah Magoffin's "noble reply" to Lincoln, in which he refused to furnish troops for the Union army. The Mayor's father, the Reverend Charles Colcock Jones Sr., sent up prayers of thankfulness that Lincoln, by his actions and declarations, had precipitated the states of the upper South to decide in favor of the Confederacy "at precisely the moment most favorable to the new nation." Jones had never believed there would be war until after Lincoln's inaugural address. The address convinced him

---

[24]Basler, *Collected Works*, 4:426
[25]Davis, *Image*, 664-66, 686-87.

that there was no justice and mercy in the President. Lincoln and his party were "arrogant, unscrupulous, intensely malignant and vitupera-tive, persecuting the innocent even unto blood and utter destruction." He prayed fervently for God's interposition to "still the tumult of the people. . . . What Lincoln . . . mean[s] to do, time only will show. We can only wait on our arms, trusting in God."[26]

Now that the war was under way, Lincoln became the target of a continual barrage of propaganda. The Southern press gave free rein to whatever vilifying and slanderous stories about Lincoln they could come by. Often the stories were preceded by such comments as: "If it be true. . . ," "An unidentified source. . . ", "A reliable source informs us. . . ." In wearisome detail the stories personified Lincoln as an oaf, a buffoon, a heartless tyrant; uncouth, ugly, given to vulgar humor. In cartoon, in verse, in melodrama, and even in musical satire, he was denounced and criticized in every conceivable fashion.[27] From their pulpits the Southern clergy denounced the enemy and their president. Both pulpit and press reviled the "black guard," Lincoln and his "currupt Congress," for wholesale violation of civil liberties. They "trampled on the United States Constitution" and "set up unlimited despotism." Ruffin, as usual, had his say, pronouncing Lincoln an "unconstitutional despot," whose Congress had given him "enormous powers."[28]

With the Fort Sumter event behind them and Yankee troops called into action, Congress began to agree on Lincoln's war objective: to restore the Union without overturning state institutions. The army would crush the rebellion and restore federal authority in the South with slavery still intact—intact in the states where it already existed. Eventually, Lincoln believed, slavery in those states would wither away. Throughout the early months of the war, Lincoln continued to maintain that his paramount object in the struggle was to save the

---

[26]Myers, *Children of Pride*, 664-66, 686-87.
[27]Davis, *Image*, 62-75; Avery Craven, "Southern Attitudes toward Abraham Lincoln," *Papers in Illinois History*. Transactions of the Illinois State Historical Society (1942), 2-18.
[28]Mitchell, *Ruffin*, 202-203; Ruffin Diary, 5 August 1862.

Union, and was neither to save nor to destroy slavery.[29] Rebel Southerners remained unconvinced. To their minds everything Lincoln said or did belied his earlier words. In truth he had entered the White House sharing in part the race prejudice of his neighbors, but the question of emancipation plagued him from the first. Often he had expressed the wish that all men everywhere should be free.[30]

Throughout Lincoln's early political life, from the time he was elected to Congress until his reelection as president, almost to the day he died, he struggled with the slave problem. At the heart of his soul-searching were his family's traditional beliefs and strict moral code. Although at heart he opposed slavery, he was reluctant to adopt stringent policies against slavery, "lest it lead to inevitable conflict" and a "violent and remorseless struggle."[31]

The violence and struggle could not be avoided. On 9 January 1861 rebels fired on Fort Sumter, initiating the Civil War. Now the very existence of a hitherto United States of America and thousands of lives were at stake. Lincoln relentlessly pursued the goal of solving the crisis and restoring the country to peaceful union. In so doing, he was subjected to barrages of criticism as he continued to perform his presidential duties. Not a formally religious man, Lincoln was never a member of a Christian church. His thought and rhetoric, however, were filled with biblical allusions and as the crush of war fell upon his shoulders, he increasingly prayed for divine guidance. On at least one occasion he said, "I am conscious every moment that all that I am and all that I have is subject to the control of a Higher Power." He also told a group of ministers who visited him near the end of 1862 that he

---

[29]Oates, *With Malice Toward None*, 322-25, 273-74; Neely, *Lincoln Encyclopedia*, 281; Frank W. Owsley, "A Southerner's View of Abraham Lincoln," *Georgia Review*, 12 (Spring 1958), 1:11-12.

[30]LaWanda Cox, *Lincoln and Black Freedom: A Study in Presidential Leadership* (Columbia: University of South Carolina Press, 1981), 19-20; William C. Davis, *The Deep Waters of the Proud*, vol. 1 *The Imperiled Union*, 1861-1865 (New York: Doubleday, 1982), 179, 286-87.

[31]David Herbert Donald, *Lincoln* (New York: Simon and Schuster, 1996), 343, 355-358, 375-376.

viewed himself as "an instrument of Providence." On another occasion, he said, "All will be well in the end, because our cause is just and God will be on our side."[32]

As the hostilities wore on, Lincoln became even more deeply sensible of his need for divine assistance. In response to harsh criticism, he endured periods of depression, incessant worry, and sleeplessness, causing his wife, Mary, to say he "looked weary, care-worn, and troubled." (See photo, facing page.) The favorable outcome of the battle of Antietam, however, convinced him of divine favor. In a turning point for the Union, on 17 September 1862 the Federals forced Lee to abandon plans for a general invasion of the North.

His spirits lifted by the turn of events and reading it as signs of God's favor, Lincoln called together his Cabinet and read to them his long-delayed proclamation of emancipation. So now with the decision made—one Lincoln believed to be right in God's eyes—he became more relaxed. He formally announced the Emancipation Proclamation, stating that on 1 January 1863, "all persons held as slaves" within any state or part of a state still in rebellion would be "thenceforth forever free." The proclamation now published, Lincoln began to receive accolades from the people of the North, to which he responded modestly that "only by trust in God had he made no mistake."[33]

In September 1862 Lincoln performed what Southerners viewed as the supreme act of tyranny. In issuing the proclamation, Lincoln claimed to be performing his duty as Commander-in-Chief—taking a nnecessary step toward crushing the enemy and saving the Union. To Confederates, however, the proclamation was the crowning act of despotism, absolute proof that his declaration of principles in the First Inaugural was deliberate deceit. Had he not repeatedly declared that his object was not to abolish slavery? The proclamation committed the nation to emancipation as a war aim. A final indignity, as seen by the South, was the President's order that blacks be enlisted in the Union armies. All the accumulated hatreds against Lincoln were now crowned

---

[32]Richard N. Current, *Lincoln Nobody Knows*, 72.
[33]Donald, *Lincoln*, 376.

The toll of four years of anxiety and overwork shows in this portrait of Lincoln by Alexander Gardner. The portrait was made a few weeks before the assassination. (The Lincoln Museum, Fort Wayne, Indiana, No. 0-118)

by an almost overpowering fear of what his proclamation would surely bring about: slave insurrection.[34]

Jefferson Davis considered the proclamation "the most execrable measure recorded in the history of guilty man [sic] perpetrated by a man who wanted to incite a race war in Dixie."[35] Less than three weeks after the Emancipation Proclamation went into effect, a Northern white regimental band led a contingent of black South Carolina Volunteers through the streets of Beaufort, indicative of changes that black leader Frederick Douglass called "vast and startling." Yet, while the number of African Americans in Union uniform grew, widespread slave insurrection did not materialize. But the fear of it remained.[36]

The *Raleigh State Journal* foresaw servile insurrection, "[A] bloody struggle between the races which would drench the South with blood." Another editor was amused when he heard that the gold pen with which Lincoln had signed the Proclamation, "the most infamous document that ever emanated from any civilized government," was being preserved "as sacredly as the sword of Washington in some museum." A better place for it, the editor opined, was Barnum's Circus Museum.[37] The *Richmond Enquirer* searched for the words for the man who mandated the preliminary Emancipation Proclamation, "What shall we call him? Coward, assassin, savage, murderer. . . ? Or shall we consider them all as embodied in the word 'fiend' and call him Lincoln, The Fiend?"[38]

Charles C. Jones, Jr., formerly Mayor of Savannah, now a Colonel in the Confederate Army, expressed the sentiments for himself and

---

[34]Leon F. Litwick, *Been in the Storm So Long: The Aftermath of Slavery* (New York: Alfred A. Knopf, 1979), 69; Hyman and Wieck, *Equal Justice*, 253-54; Richard Bardolf, "Malice Toward One—Lincoln in the North Carolina Press," *Lincoln Herald* 53 (Winter, 1952) 4:43; *Fayetteville Semi-Weekly Observer*, October 27, 1862.

[35]Stephen B. Oates, *Abraham Lincoln: The Man Behind the Myth* (New York: Harper & Row, 1984), 18.

[36]Litwack, *Been in the Storm*, 526-528.

[37]*Raleigh Weekly Journal*, 8 October 1862; *Raleigh Semi-Weekly Standard*, October 3, 1862; Bardolf, "Malice Toward One," *Lincoln Herald* 53 4:44; Litwack, 69.

[38]*Richmond Enquirer*, 21 October 1862; Herbert Mitgang, *Lincoln as They Saw Him* (New York: Rhinehard, 1957), 324.

other slave-owning Georgians when he declared that Lincoln's latest "act" showed the same heartless fanaticism with which he first began the war. He complained:

This latest diabolical transaction marked the entire course of his administration. I look upon it as a direct bid for insurrection, as a most infamous attempt to incite flight, murder, and rapine on the part of our slave population. [We] are beset with perils which humanity in its worst phases has not encountered for centuries.

Jones further declared that the "infamous Lincoln" by his proclamation intended to "subvert our entire social system, desolate our homes, and convert the quiet, ignorant black son of toil into a savage, incendiary and brutal murderer. . . ."[39]

Throughout 1863 and 1864, as blood continued to be shed on both sides of the conflict and into his second term as president, he rededicated his efforts to, as he had said in the Gettysburg Address, "the great task remaining before us . . . that these dead shall not have died in vain; that his nation under God shall have a new birth of freedom, and the government of the people, by the people, and for the people shall not perish from the earth."[40]

During 1864, Lincoln's armies became increasingly successful, and after Sherman's capture of Atlanta, there was little doubt that the president would be reelected. On 18 January 1865, Lincoln let it be known to his self-appointed advisor, elder statesman Francis P. Blair, that he was ready to receive any Southern agent "with the view of securing peace to the people of our common country." Blair met with Jefferson Davis in private, and although Davis thought reconciliation of North and South was all but impossible, he showed interest in a conference between representatives of both sides. A meeting was arranged. Lincoln received Davis's peace commissioners on a steamer

---

[39]Myers, *Children of Pride,* 967,997.
[40]Current, *Lincoln Nobody Knows,* 250-251.

anchored off Fortress Monroe. Neither side was willing to compromise; the conference ended without result.[41]

Davis angrily reported the collapse of the conference to his Congress and his people. He saw its failure as one more instance of Lincoln's intractible hostility; just one more example of his determination to conquer and exterminate the people of the South. Davis's fiery words added more fuel to the already crackling flames of hatred toward Lincoln.[42]

The editor of the Petersburg, Virginia, *Daily Express* denounced what he considered the ostentatious pageantry of Lincoln's second inauguration. "With a soul loaded down with the guilt of wholesale murder, robbery and arson," he wrote, Lincoln was guilty of "the greatest and blackest catalogue of offenses against God, his country, and humanity, that one man on the American continent could present for the world's abhorrence."[43] Similar pronouncements appeared in the columns of other Southern papers.

Despite these scathing attacks, Lincoln never spoke in bitter terms toward the South. There was, indeed, no word of harshness in the President's Second Inaugural Address, which admonished:

> With malice toward none; with charity for all; with firmness in the right, as God gives us to see the right, let us strive on to finish the work we are in; to bind up the nation's wounds; to care for him who shall have borne the battle, and for his widow, and his orphan—to do all which may achieve and cherish a just and lasting peace among ourselves, and with all nations.[44]

---

[41]Neely, *Lincoln Encyclopedia*, 29-30; Davis, *Image*, 95-97.

[42]Edward Albert Pollard, *Life of Jefferson Davis, with Secret History of the Southern Confederacy, Gathered behind the Scenes in Richmond* (Philadelphia: National Printing Company, 1968), 471.

[43]*Petersburg (Virginia) Daily Express*, 4 March 1865.

[44]J. G. deRoulhac Hamilton, "Lincoln and the South," *Sewanee Review*, 17 (April, 1909), 130-32.

Five and a half weeks later, on Friday evening, 14 April 1865, John Wilkes Booth, a disgruntled and unstable Southern actor, shot the president as he sat in Ford's Theatre in Washington. Early next morning, the President died. Another Good Friday had claimed another martyr.

"Some will regard it with all the horror of the most wicked assassination," the editor of a Texas newspaper wrote. Others, however, "will feel it to be that righteous retribution which descends direct from the hand of God upon the destroyer of human liberty, and the oppressor of a free people."

John Wilkes Booth, Lincoln's assassin
(The Lincoln Museum, Fort Wayne, Indiana, No. 3527)

Chapter 2

Reaction in
the Upper South

A church bell sounded a prolonged and mournful knell. Another followed and then another, until the sound echoed throughout the city of Washington. Cannon fire soon joined the clamor. The sound of bells cut through the rain all that day and all night long. Cannon thundered every half hour. As the hours passed, the people of Washington learned the cause of the clanging bells and the booming cannon. All came to believe the unbelievable: President Lincoln lay dead, killed by an assassin's bullet. Some were speechless, white-faced and grim; many wept, rain and tears mingled on their cheeks; others swore to the heavens, their faces livid with rage. "Damn the rebels, it is their work!" swore Secretary of the Navy Gideon Wells when he heard the news. It was the common reaction of most citizens of Washington.[1]

In the night, Secretary of War Edwin M. Stanton had rushed to the Peterson house where Lincoln lay dying. In charge of matters that terrible night, Stanton moved to the President's bedside in the early morning. He wept quietly as Lincoln died. After the lifeless body was removed to the White House, Stanton remained briefly and composed a telegram to General John Adams Dix, at his headquarters in New York:

Washington City,
April 15, 1865

---

[1]Thomas Reed Turner, *Beware the People Weeping, Public Opinion and the Assassination of Lincoln* (Baton Rouge: Louisiana State University Press, 1982), 46.

Major General Dix
New York

Abraham Lincoln died this morning at 22 minutes after 7 o'clock.

Edwin M. Stanton
Secretary of War[2]

The *New York Herald* announced in black-bordered columns "The President is Dead," with the dispatch from Stanton to Dix appearing beneath the headline. Similar telegraphic messages were published throughout the cities of the North. Commanders of the occupying forces throughout the South also received official dispatches. But Stanton directed the officers-in-charge of Southern posts to withhold the news from their troops for a few days. He feared the news would cause angry reprisals against the Southerners.[3]

In Washington five days later, after funeral services had been held in the White House, bells again tolled continuously as the slain President was borne in procession from the White House to the Capitol. (See photo, facing page.) For more than two hours the bells sounded their funereal measures, bands played dirges, and drums beat a muffled cadence as columns of mourners moved slowly down the avenue to the Capitol. A detachment of black troops was first in the procession. Following the coffin, thousands of black citizens, forty abreast, took their places in line after government dignitaries and delegations of citizens of Northern states. Battalions of soldiers, the clergy, maimed veterans, school children wearing badges, and members of benevolent societies and associations made up the remainder of the solemn procession. Many more grieving citizens paid their respects to the slain President after his body had been placed on the catafalque in

---

[2]Jim Bishop, *The Day Lincoln Was Shot* (New York: Harper and Brothers, 1955), 295-97; Stephen B. Oates, *With Malice Toward None: The Life of Abraham Lincoln* (New York: New American Library Edition, 1977), 470-474.

[3]William Hanchett, *The Lincoln Murder Conspiracies* (Chicago: University of Illinois Press, 1953), 59-60.

President Lincoln's funeral procession in Washington, D.C.
(The Lincoln Museum, Fort Wayne, Indiana, No. 4483)

the Capitol's rotunda.[4]

Bells on the engine of the nine-car train were set to ringing when, on 22 April, Lincoln's coffin was placed aboard the train for his last journey from the capitol to his home in Illinois. Along the route, through city after city—New York, Cleveland, Indianapolis, Chicago—the train bells announced the arrival of the funeral cars. Thousands viewed the coffin in the statehouse in Albany, others paid homage to him throughout Ohio, Michigan, Pennsylvania. Where there were no stops planned, mute crowds stood in the rain as the train moved slowly by them.[5]

Throughout the North, overt expressions of shock and grief and mourning were widespread. Although Southerners were shocked by the crime and abhorred the murder, there were few expressions of unrestrained grief for the President. When the commanding officers of the occupying forces of Southern cities or towns received announcements of the assassination, they used their own judgment about when and how to release the news. In many instances they ordered bells to be tolled, announcements to be made, and eulogizing editorials to be printed within black-bordered columns of the local newspapers. Upon orders from Washington, they directed that a day of mourning be observed, that sermons be preached, businesses be closed, and public buildings be draped in black. On flagpoles where the Stars and Stripes had recently replaced the Stars and Bars, the poles were to be covered in black.[6]

Confederate President Jefferson Davis and his cabinet had fled the Confederate capital by the time of Lincoln's death. Following the receipt of Stanton's dispatch, General Edward Ord, now commander-in-charge of Richmond, withheld the news from his troops for a few days, and official reports and details of the assassination did not appear

---

[4]*Charleston Courier*, 26 April 1865. Reprinted from the *New York Times*, 20 April 1865; *New York Herald*, 29 April 1865.

[5]Oates, *With Malice Toward None*, 473-474.

[6]*Charleston Courier*, 20-21 April 1965: *Savannah Morning News*, 20-22 April 1865; *New Orleans Times*, 22 April 1865.

in Richmond newspapers as promptly as they did in the *New York Herald* and other Union newspapers.

In Richmond, rebel war clerk John B. Jones had served his government well under five Confederate Secretaries of War. When President Davis, his cabinet, and entourage left in the night for a safer place in the deep South, they left clerk Jones to the mercies of the Yankees. They had no room for him and his family on the train headed for the Carolinas. Jones was stuck in Richmond, trying desperately to obtain permission from General Ord to leave the city with his family. Jones was still there on 17 April, two days after Lincoln's death, when he heard rumors of the assassination, and added some lines to his diary:

> It was whispered, yesterday, that President Lincoln had been assassinated! I met Gen. Duff Green, in the afternoon, who assured me there could be no doubt about it. Still, supposing it might be an April hoax, I inquired at the headquarters of Gen. Ord, and was told it was true. I cautioned those I met to manifest no *feeling*, as the occurrence might be a calamity for the South; and possibly the Federal soldiers, supposing the deed to have been done by a Southern man, might become uncontrollable and perpetrate deeds of Horror on the unarmed people. . . . I suppose [the assassin's] purpose is to live in history as the slayer of a tyrant; thinking to make the leading character in a tragedy, and have his performance acted by others on the stage.[7]

Mary Custis Lee was at home in Richmond when she received word of the assassination. For the general's wife, there had been months of weary wandering, living with kind relatives and friends while her husband commanded the Confederate Army, "I cannot believe there is any truth to it," she said, as did numerous other Richmond people who

---

[7]John B. Jones, *A Rebel War Clerk's Diary*, Earl Schenck Miers, ed. (New York: A. S. Barnes Company, Inc., 1961), ix, 536, 538.

had got word of the assassination in spite of Stanton's orders to withhold the news for a few days.[8]

Lucy Fletcher, a Richmond minister's wife, also heard the "horrible rumor" that Lincoln had been slain. Next day, when she realized "it is even so," she felt it was one of the most startling tragedies ever enacted in real life. It must have been the work of a lunatic, she believed, for certainly no judicious friend of the South could "hope for an improvement under Andy Johnson." Many who were lukewarm before, Lucy felt, would now feel sympathy for Lincoln as a martyr, a sympathy which "Lincoln, the buffoon, would never have created." Lucy heard terrible accounts of riots in the North as a consequence of Lincoln's murder, for which Southern sympathizers would be injuriously affected. Remorse filled her heart for the assassin who, in performing one of the "most daring acts on record," must have been prompted by a heart "wrung to desperation by some of the tyrannical deeds of Lincoln and his government."[9]

Another Richmond woman, Susanna Gordon Waddell, was less concerned about the assassin than about the consequences of his deed. "Oh Lord," she asked, "How long wilt thou be angry with us? The death of Lincoln is far from being desirable for us. [It] seems now to have been the worst thing that could have happened to us." Resignedly, she added, "But the Lord knows best."[10]

Similar to other Richmond women, Judith McGuire felt free to reveal her true reaction to the assassination only to her diary. General Ord had issued an order for Richmond citizens to pray for President Lincoln. On the Sunday the order appeared in the newspaper, there were no services in Judith's church. "How could we do it?" she

---

[8]Katherine Jones, *Heroines of Dixie* (New York: Bobby-Merrill Company, 1955), 403-404; Mrs. R. E. Lee to Louisa Snowden. Typed copy of a letter dated 18 April 1865, Lloyd House Library, Alexandria, Virginia.

[9]Lucy Muse (Walton) Fletcher Papers, 1816-1968. Manuscript Department, William R. Perkins Library, Duke University. Diary entries dated 18, 19, and 22 April 1865.

[10]Susannah Gordon Waddell Diary, entry dated 22 April 1865, Waddell Papers, Southern Historical Collection, University of North Carolina, Chapel Hill.

lamented. "Thank God, our private prayers are free from Federal authority."[11] Cornelia McDonald was also in Richmond during the days following Lincoln's death. At first, she thought the "taking off" of Lincoln was just what he deserved; that he had urged on and promoted the savage war that cost so many lives. But on reflection, she saw that it was worse for the South than if he had been allowed to live. At least Lincoln had a merciful side to him. Cornelia expected no mercy from Lincoln's successor, Andrew Johnson, or from a "nation of infuriated fanatics whose idol of clay had been cast down." Cornelia expected that the Southern people would be accused of planning the murder and procuring its execution. She was convinced that vengeance would be taken and that the crime would be visited upon Southern leaders.[12]

Perhaps Myrta Lockett Avary was most direct and apt of all the Richmond women who expressed reaction to the assassination:

I heard some speak who thought it no more than just retribution upon Mr. Lincoln for the havoc he had wrought in our country. But even the few who spoke thus were horrified when details came. We could not be expected to grieve, from any sense of personal affection for Mr. Lincoln, whom we had seen only in the position of an implacable foe at the head of a power invading and devastating our land; but our reprobation of the crime of his taking off was none the less. Besides, we did not know what would be done to us. Already there had been talk of trying our officers for treason, of executing them, of exiling them and in this talk Andrew Johnson had been loudest.

I remember how one poor woman took the news. She was half-crazed by her losses and troubles; one son had been killed in battle, another had died in prison, of another she could not hear if he were living or dead; her house had been burned; her

[11][Dorothy Brockenbrough McGuire] *Diary of a Southern Refugee During the Civil War by a Lady of Virginia* (New York: E. J. Hale & Son, 1868), 355-356, entry for 17 April 1865; Jones, *Heroines*, 399-400.

[12]Cornelia McDonald. *A Diary with Reminiscences of the War and Refugee Life, 1860-1865* (Nashville, Tennessee: Cullom & Ghertner Co., 1934), 260.

young daughter, turned out with her in the night, had died of fright and exposure. She ran in, crying: "Lincoln has been killed! Thank God!" Next day she came, still and pale: "I have prayed it all out of my heart," she said. "[T]hat is, I'm not glad. But, somehow, I *can't* be sorry, I believe it was the vengeance of the Lord."[13]

A number of Richmond ministers struggled with their consciences when faced with the necessity of holding special services on the day of prayer set aside by President Johnson for the death of Lincoln. They came up with various solutions to the problem of being required to eulogize the slain President in their pulpits, when genuine words of praise stuck in their throats. Dr. J. L. Burrows of the First Baptist Church of Richmond took the opportunity to pray for the punishment of the guilty, at the same time vehemently denying the guilt of the South:

> It has been said that the South should be held responsible for the assassination of President Lincoln, and that severe measures should be adopted toward the people because of this crime. . . . This would be, in its turn, an injustice and crime. To hold a whole people responsible for an outrage which they not only disown, but deplore and abhor, might be the first impulse of blind and phrenzied passion, but cannot become a principle of action with fairminded and magnanimous men. Let the guilty suffer. . . . [But] in the name of the South, I protest . . . against being involved in the remotest degree in an atrocity from which my whole soul revolts, and which can awaken no utterance of more honest and indignant condemnation in any section of the country, than in these Southern States.[14]

---

[13]Myrta Lockett Avary, *Dixie* i, 83

[14]*New York Times*, 1 May 1865. As quoted in Martin Abbot, "Southern Reaction to Lincoln's Assassination," *Abraham Lincoln Quarterly*, 7 (September, 1952) 3:124.

Another Richmond minister found only five or six persons in the congregation who would gather for the required memorial service. Hattie Blenheim, one of the congregants, later wrote that when the minister spoke from the pulpit, he said,

My friends, we have been ordered to meet here by those in authority for humiliation and prayer on account of the death of Lincoln. Having met, we will now be dismissed with the doxology: "Praise God from whom all blessings flow!"[15]

From his post in a tobacco warehouse in Petersburg, Virginia, Union General George L. Hartsuff observed the rebel prisoners around him. Having learned with deep regret of the President's death, he watched rebel behavior with a keen eye when he publicized the news. He confided to his journal that he had no doubt that many a rebel soldier regretted Lincoln's death.[16]

The Union guards were doubled and the soldiers looked angry and vindictive the morning the news arrived at the prison camp at Fort Delaware. W. H. Morgan, a Virginian and a Confederate officer who had been held prisoner at the fort for almost a year, immediately had visions of retaliatory measures on the part of the guards. But no such act occurred. Weeks later, after Morgan had been released and was safely at his father's Virginia home twenty-one miles from Lynchburg, he came to the conclusion that the assassination of Lincoln was the act of a scatter-brained lunatic, who did the South no good. Although Morgan thought many people believed that if Lincoln had lived the South would have fared better; he himself did not think so. Lincoln might have been disposed to deal more justly with the South, but in Morgan's view he would have been "overruled by the Sewards, the Stantons, the Mortons, the Garrisons, and the Thad Stevenses, and

---

[15]Hattie Powell Blenheim to Nina Powell, 15 June 1865, Powell Family Papers, Manuscript Department, Swem Library, College of William and Mary, Williamsburg, Virginia.

[16]Major General George F. Hartsuff Journal, entry of 27 April 1865, Special Collections, Woodruff Library, Emory University, Atlanta, Georgia.

many more of that ilk, who lived and died inveterate haters and vilifiers of the Southern people." "Meanness," he continued in his diary, "is bred in the bone of some people. If Lincoln ever did a kindly or generous a ct in behalf of the South, I do not recall it."[17]

In the cabinet car of his train, Jefferson Davis and the remnants of his fleeing Confederate government continued South from Richmond, through Danville, Greensboro, Lexington, Salisbury, Concord, and Charlotte, North Carolina. Davis and his train arrived in Charlotte ten days after the North had celebrated Grant's victory and the South had generally accepted their defeat. In Charlotte, Davis hoped to reestablish the government, still clinging to the forlorn hope of reviving the Confederacy. Even as Confederate General Joseph E. Johnston was carrying out the orders of the cabinet to negotiate the surrender of his army and to ask General William Tecumseh Sherman for peace, Davis could not bring himself to believe that the Confederacy was dead.[18]

Johnston was one of the first Confederate officers to learn of Lincoln's death. At noon on 17 April, near Durham, North Carolina, General Johnston was to meet with Sherman. Halfway between the pickets of the two armies, Johnston rode with his cavalry chief, General Wade Hampton and Major General John C. Breckinridge, who was Confederate Secretary of War. Sherman with members of his staff rode from the opposite direction. When the parties met, they shook hands and continued on their way, Johnston and Sherman riding side by side. When they neared a small log house, the two officers dismounted and approached the house together. The mistress of the house, Lucy Bennett, met them at the door, granting them permission to use her home for their conference. She gathered her children together and took them to a small house in the yard. The men entered, and Sherman

---

[17]W. H. Morgan, *Personal Reminiscences of the War of 1861-1865* (Lynchburg, Virginia: J. P. Bell and Company, 1911), 267-270.

[18]A. J. Hanna, *Flight into Oblivion* (Richmond: Johnson Publishing Company, 1938), 46-49.

closed the door behind them. Out of sight of the others, Sherman pulled a paper from his pocket and handed it to Johnston. More lengthy than the dispatch Stanton had sent to General Dix moments after Lincoln's death, this telegram, after explaining that an assassin had shot Lincoln "through the head by a pistol ball," indicated that Vice President Andrew Johnson "now becomes President." Stanton ended the dispatch with a warning to Sherman:

> I have no time to add more than to say I find evidence that an assassin is also on your track, and I beseech you to be more heedful than Mr. Lincoln was of such knowledge.[19]

Sherman watched General Johnston closely as he read the message, as large drops of perspiration appeared on his forehead and his face reddened. In strong language Johnston denounced the assassination as a "disgrace to the age." Immediately, he told Sherman he hoped he "did not charge it to the Confederate Government." Sherman assured Johnston that he, personally, did not. The two generals discussed the effect of Lincoln's murder on the country at large and on the two opposing armies. Sherman explained to Johnston that he had not yet revealed the news to his own staff, nor to the army; nor had it been announced in Raleigh. Sherman particularly dreaded the effect once he made Lincoln's assassination known in Raleigh. He feared that his soldiers, to whom Lincoln was "peculiarly endeared," would inflict a fate on the place *"worse* than that of Columbia," which had been pillaged and burned by Union forces. Johnston equally feared retaliation on *all* citizens of the South.[20]

---

[19]Gilbert G. Govan and James A. Livingston, *A Different Valor: The Story of General Joseph E. Johnston, C.S.A.* (Indianapolis, Indiana: Bobbs-Merrill, 1956), 363-365; William C. Davis, *Breckinridge, Statesman, Soldier, Symbol* (Baton Rouge: Louisiana State University Press, 1976), 513-514.

[20]Phillip van Doren Stern, *An End to Valor: The Last Days of the Civil War* (Boston: Houghton Mifflin, 1958), 323-325;Emma LeConte Diary, Southern Historical Collection, entry dated 14 April 1865.

Breckinridge was then called into the house, and the three men discussed the grave matter for which they had come together. They agreed on terms of armistice. But the two Confederate officers explained that they did not have control over all of the subjects embraced in the agreement, and they pledged themselves to secure that authority from the proper sources.[21] Before the generals joined the others outside the house, Sherman and Johnston told Breckinridge of Lincoln's assassination. Breckinridge, stunned at the news, had been on friendly terms with Lincoln even though the men had been political opponents. Breckinridge considered it a strange coincidence that he had lived in the Peterson boarding house when he was a congressman—the very house, perhaps the very room in which Lincoln had died. Lincoln had in the past regretted that Breckinridge "had sided with the South." Now that his friend was dead, Breckinridge murmured, "Gentlemen, the South has lost its best friend."[22]

That night after he returned to Raleigh, Sherman officially announced Lincoln's death. The news caused a great stir among the Union troops, many of whom swore "eternal *vengeance* against the *whole* Southern race." Sherman was able to cool the violent reactions among the men by instructing the general in command to carry out certain special orders and precautions to safeguard the city. The offices of the Confederate newspapers in Raleigh had been promptly wrecked when Sherman first entered the city four days earlier. The Raleigh *Progress,* which had been suspended, was permitted to resume publication once editor William Holden agreed to toe the Union line.[23]

Charlotte had also fallen to Sherman. It was no wonder that when Jefferson Davis arrived in Charlotte and directed that quarters be found

---

[21]D. S. Lamont, ed. *War of the Rebellion: Official Records of the Union and Confederate Armies* (Washington, D.C.: Government Printing Office, 1895), Ser. I, Vol. 42, Pt. 3, 243; William T. Sherman, *Memoirs,* vol. 2 (New York, 1876), 357.

[22]Davis, *Breckinridge,* 451; Richard E. Yates, "Governor Vance and the End of the War in North Carolina," *North Carolina Historical Review,* 18 (October 1941) 4:315; John G. Barrett, *The Civil War in North Carolina Press,* 1963), 380-383.

[23]W. C. Meffert Diary, entry dated 18 April 1865, State Historical Society of Wisconsin, Madison, Wisconsin.

for him only one house was offered, and that reluctantly by a convivial bachelor named Bates. General George Stoneman's cavalry had threatened to burn the house of anyone who acted as host to the Confederate President. Davis was standing on the steps of the Bates house with William Johnson, a Charlotte businessman who had come to greet him, when a telegraph agent ran through the crowd that had gathered and handed Davis a dispatch from his Secretary of War that read:

April 19, 1865

His Excellency, President Davis:

President Lincoln was assassinated in the theatre in Washington. . . . Seward's house was entered . . . and [he] is probably mortally wounded.

John C. Breckinridge

Davis read the words, read them a second time, then quietly conveyed the message to those around him. "It is sad news," he said as he handed the paper to Johnson. At that moment, a column of Kentucky cavalry galloped into the street, waving flags and hurrahing for Davis. Some halted at the steps and called for a speech. Davis responded, spoke brief words in compliment of their gallantry, and urged them not to despair, to remain with the last organized band upholding the Confederate flag. Davis asked Johnson to read the telegram to the crowd. One among them shouted with joy when he heard the words; others would have cheered, but Davis silenced them with an upraised hand, turned, and passed into the house. The crowd dispersed in silence.[24]

---

[24]Hudson Strode, *Jefferson Davis, Tragic Hero: The Last Twenty-Five Years, 1865-1889* (New York: Harcourt Brace, 1964), 192-193. Ishbel Ross, *First Lady of the South, the Life of Mrs. Jefferson Davis* (New York: Harper and Brothers, 1958), 227; Michael Davis, *Image of Lincoln*, 21-22, 100-103.

Stephen R. Mallory, Secretary of the Navy in Davis's Cabinet, was not with Davis when he received the dispatch from Breckinridge, but he heard the news a few minutes later. When Mallory expressed his utter disbelief to Davis, Davis replied that in times of revolution, events no less startling were constantly occurring. Mallory was sure of Lincoln's moderation and his sense of justice, but he was extremely apprehensive that the South would be accused of instigating his death. To this Davis replied sadly, "I certainly had no special regard for Mr. Lincoln, but there are a great many men of whose end I would much rather have heard than his. I fear it will be disastrous to our people, and I regret it deeply."[25] Many years later Davis recorded his thoughts about Lincoln:

> For an enemy so relentless in the war for our subjugation, we could not be expected to mourn yet, in view of its political consequences, it could not be regarded otherwise than as a great misfortune to the South. He had power over the Northern people, and was without personal malignity toward the people of the South. His successor [Johnson of Tennessee] was without power in the North, and the embodiment of malignity toward the Southern people, perhaps the more so because he had betrayed and deserted them in the hour of their need.[26]

Alexander H. Stephens, Vice President of the Confederacy, "thought well of" Lincoln personally. Back in the late 1840s, Stephens and Lincoln learned to respect each other as members of the House of Representatives. Destined to become mighty adversaries, the two nevertheless developed a mutual regard for each other, although their opinions and principles were worlds apart. Stephens was deeply affected

---

[25]Stephen Mallory Diary, entry dated 19 April 1865, Southern Historical Collection, University of North Carolina, Chapel Hill; Stephen P. Mallory, "Last Days of the Confederate Government," *McClure Magazine* 16 (2902) 242-243.

[26]Jefferson Davis, *The Rise and Fall of the Confederate Government* (New York, 1881), 2:683

by Lincoln's death, and throughout the years of war and reconstruction Stephens continued to believe that with Lincoln as president, the South would have been safe if it had not seceded and would have been safer returning to the Union if Lincoln had lived.[27] Stephens' views were shared by a North Carolinian named Schenck, who wrote in his journal:

> I forgot in this hurried resumé to mention the assassination of Lincoln and the enthroning of Andy Johnson as President of the United States, which though viewed in many aspects was to us politically disastrous, as old Abe with all his apeishness was a kindhearted man disposed to treat us generously and mercifully. . . . The South too feels specially galled at the power of Andy Johnson, who as a renegade, demagogue, and drunkard is peculiarly intolerable to them.[28]

Charles S. Brown of the 21st Infantry, Michigan Volunteers, had the pleasure of hoisting the Stars and Stripes over Raleigh when Governor Zebulon Vance surrendered not only the city, but the entire State of North Carolina. Brown joined his fellow Yankees in cheering "three times three and a tiger" when his division received the announcement of Lee's surrender. His exuberant shouts quickly changed to sputtering anger when he heard of Lincoln's murder:

> May the Lord have mercy upon the Country we pass through and the Rebels we catch. . . . [F]ew men will stop from committing any outrage or crime they may wish to. . . . I would

---

[27]Michael Davis, *Image of Lincoln*, 21-23; 100-103; Myrta L. Avary, ed., *Recollections of Alexander H. Stephens: His Diary Kept When a Prisoner at Fort Warren, Boston Harbor, 1865* (New York: Doubleday, 1910), 21-22, 276; Abbott, "Southern Reaction," *Lincoln Quarterly* 7 (September 1952) 3:113; Hudson Strode, *Tragic Hero* 219; Richard Malcolm Johnston and William Hand Brown, *Life of Alexander H. Stephens* (Philadelphia, 1884), 624.

[28]Schenck Papers. Southern Historical Collection, University of North Carolina at Chapel Hill. Schenck Journal, typed copy. April [n.d.] 1865.

like to see Wm [Sherman] turn his army loose over what is left.
. . . [The assassination] is the worst news we have ever heard
yet. I hope Andrew Johnson will put down the screws tight[;]
by thunder the army will sustain him if it hangs every man &
burns every house in the whole South.

A Wisconsin soldier upon reading the official news in the *Raleigh
Standard* agreed wholeheartedly with the Michigan Volunteer. He
swore vengeance against the whole Southern people, and some of his
buddies proposed to begin with Raleigh—to burn the city down and
kill every rebel in it.[29]

Dr. William Lomax, a Union medical officer, saw his worst fears
materialize when he witnessed the hissings and cursings of the Union
soldiers against the people of Raleigh in the wake of Lincoln's murder.
Lomax also observed first hand how the people of Raleigh reacted to
the news. He observed that the ex-rebels seemed to feel the death of
Lincoln

as keenly as the loyal people; and he was sure that *they* will
suffer greater calamity in all probability *than we*. . . . They have
less confidence in the clemency of Andy Johnson than they had
in Lincoln. Johnson . . . is a more vindictive man.

As for his fellow soldiers, Lomax observed that they were struck with
a feeling of unbounded revenge, a feeling that the townspeople
immediately sensed, so that they were "afraid to venture upon the
streets." Guards were trebled and soldiers patrolled all the streets of
Raleigh. Under the strict military commands of the Union officers,
disorder and loud vindictiveness soon gave place to a stillness as if the
"shadow of death had fallen on the troops." The town became
extremely quiet. Raleigh was quieted by military order. Other towns

---

[29]Charles S. Brown to Mother and Etta, 18 April 1865, Charles S. Brown Papers,
Manuscript Department, Duke University Library, Durham, NC; Bell Irvin Wiley,
"Billy Yank and Abraham Lincoln," *Abraham Lincoln Quarterly*, 6 (June 1950), 2:119.

were not so fortunate. Where occupying forces were encamped when the news of Lincoln's murder arrived, pillagings, burnings, and shootings occurred.[30]

Lomax accurately assessed the feelings of his fellow Yankees; he was also right in observing that the rebels "seemed" to feel the death of Lincoln keenly. Like the women of Richmond, the women of Raleigh and Charlotte kept their inmost thoughts to themselves, expressing them only to each other behind drawn curtains and closed doors or in their journals and diaries. When rumors were rife and later when official announcements came, families remained indoors as much as possible. When the orders came to observe a day of mourning, the townspeople dutifully complied, hanging whatever black cloth they could find—often an old coat or pants—over their windows and lintel posts. In Charlotte, Raleigh, Wilmington, New Bern—in other North Carolina towns, large and small—the citizens were called upon to mourn the late President. The day of mourning, by order, "will not be one of mere empty demonstration," the Wilmington *Herald of the Union* declared. In fear of severe reprisal if they did not obey, at least on the *face* of it, the order was strictly obeyed.[31]

So it was that a large congregation was present in the small Methodist Church in Lumberton, North Carolina, for Sunday services at which the Reverend Washington Chaffin would preach. On orders from the Commander (Union cavalry had come to Lumberton only the Friday before) the people gathered on Sunday to observe the day in mourning for the slain President and in prayer for the new leader, Andrew Johnson. Chaffin was a circuit rider who throughout the war years had travelled by horse and buggy, or had mounted his horse and taken his message to small congregations throughout the countryside in Robeson County, North Carolina. On numerous Sundays he drew his themes for his sermons from current events of the war, referring to

---

[30]Letter, William Lomax to Dr. A.W. Reese, typed copy dated 23 April 1865. William Lomax Papers, Joint Collection of Missouri Western Historical Manuscript Collection, Columbia and State Historical Society of Missouri Manuscripts.

[31]*Wilmington Herald of the Union*, 16 April 1865; *(New Bern) North Carolina Times*, 18 April 1865.

pertinent passages of scripture, drawing analogies from them for his listeners. When Lee surrendered to Grant, he commented that it meant "a virtual ending of the great war; alas that it was continued so long!" On the Sunday observed as a day of mourning in Lumberton, Chaffin preached an especially moving sermon, including the words, "Every good and sensible man deprecates the murder of President Lincoln." In his closing prayer, Chaffin prayed that there may be "no more sectional animosity; that the new President have the pity of Josiah, his counselors the wisdom of Aristophil [sic], that wrath and hatred and all malice be laid aside; that there be no more wasting and destruction." Later, a baffled Chaffin learned that members of his congregation had taken exception to his remarks.[32]

On the day designated for mourning, Reverend George M. Everhart, Rector of St. Peter's Church in Charlotte, preached to a congregation composed of Jefferson Davis, members of his cabinet, Union military notables, and prominent North Carolina citizens, "the like of which Charlotte had never seen before." The rector preached vigorously, characterizing the assassination as a

> blot on American civilization, which in this nineteenth century of the Christian era is doubly deep in infamy. . . . [T]his event, unjustifiable at any time, but occurring just now, renders it obligatory upon every Christian to set his face against it—to express his abhorrence of a deed fraught with consequences to society everywhere, and more especially to Southern society.

Davis listened, bemused, and after the service, as he left the church, remarked with a smile, "I think the preacher directed his remarks to me; and he really seems to fancy I had something to do with the assassination."[33]

---

[32]Washington Sandford Chaffin Papers. Manuscript Department, Duke University Library, "Brief Journal," April and May, 1865.

[33]A. J. Hanna, *Flight Into Oblivion* (Richmond, Virginia: Johnson Publishing Company, 1938), 47-48.

In Arkansas, as in North Carolina, some regretted Lincoln's demise, others rejoiced; many upon hearing of Lincoln's death felt anxiety and fright. Federal troops entered Little Rock a few months before Lincoln's death, and a Unionists had held a convention that repudiated secession and abolished slavery. The editor of the Little Rock *Daily Gazette*, a native of Arkansas, had edited his paper "until the announcement of war." Shortly after the assassination, he resumed editorship in the hope of serving the people "among whom we were raised and the country to which our allegiance is [now] due." Official mourning days were observed in relative calm, and the editor adherred to his stated course:

> to sustain the civil authorities; to labor to bring about a feeling of confidence, faith, and security among the people . . . to inculcate love and trust among all good citizens . . . to induce forgetfulness of the dead and bad past.[34]

The citizens of Tennessee, with its large Unionist population, had widely diverse reactions to the assassination. Slavery was of relatively less economic importance in Tennessee and the rate of blacks-to-whites was much smaller than in the states of the deep South. There were also many who believed that a "natural antagonism" existed between the richer, slave-owning classes and the poorer classes, and that the poorer classes lacked leadership in the South. But in Tennessee, where at least a quarter of the people were utterly impoverished, the poor found their leader in the person of Andrew Johnson. Born in Raleigh, North Carolina, he moved as a young man to East Tennessee, living among others of his kind, where the plantation-slavery aristocracy was outnumbered by the small farmer. Although he defended slavery and owned a few slaves himself. During the Civil War, however, Johnson remained a rabid Unionist, sharing with Lincoln the passionate desire to liberate East Tennessee from the powerful rich whom he furiously

---

[34]William E. Wight, ed. "The Bishop of Natchez on the Death of Lincoln," *Lincoln Herald,* 58 (Fall 1956), 13-14; *Little Rock Gazette,* 10 May 1865.

opposed. Because of his staunch stand for the Union, he retained his seat in the U.S. Senate, even though his state had seceded. (He was the only member of Congress from a seceding state to remain in Congress.) After Union troops overran parts of Tennessee, Lincoln appointed Johnson Military Governor of the state. Because of Johnson's diligence in that capacity, and because he would help broaden the appeal of the ticket, Lincoln made him his running mate in 1864. Booth's bullet elevated Andrew Johnson to the Presidency.[35]

Like Johnson, William G. Brownlow grew up in the mountains of Tennessee in poverty. "Parson" Brownlow despised "Andy" Johnson, but the two shared Union leadership in East Tennessee. For ten years during his young manhood, the "fighting Parson" ranged up and down the state, expounding not only upon the saving of souls, but upon saving Tennessee from the secessionists, upon keeping the state safe within the Union. Though he was no abolitionist, he was an adamant Unionist, and he preached that gospel not only during the years he was a Methodist Circuit rider, but later in his life when he turned his talents from the ministry to journalism. He was so outspoken in his newspapers (first the Jonesboro *Whig*, later the Knoxville *Whig*) in championing the Union and President Lincoln, and in opposing the Confederacy, that he was thrown into prison by the Confederate government in 1862. Upon his release, he fled to the North where he freely lectured on the Union cause. After most of Tennessee came under Union control, Brownlow returned to Knoxville and happily resumed editorship of the *Whig* under his former pro-Unionist policy. When Lincoln took Johnson as his running mate in 1864, Lincoln approved of Brownlow's replacement of Johnson as Governor of Tennessee. Upon assuming office, Brownlow hired a businessman with Union sympathies to "take care of internal affairs" of his newspaper, and he continued to fill the columns of his newspaper with verbal ammunition, aimed at the "Constitutional conservative, fence-riding, half-horse, and half-alegator [sic] men of East Tennessee. . . . those hell-deserving persecutors of Union families."

---

[35]Mark Neely, Jr., *Lincoln Encyclopedia,* 64, 164-168, 231.

In black-bordered columns in the *Whig* issue of 19 April 1865, Brownlow wrote,

> With profound sadness we announce the death of Abraham Lincoln—an event which will startle the world. . . . The sad end of Mr. Lincoln, at the very moment when all men were inclining to mercy and forgiveness, will arouse afresh a stern spirit of indignation and call up the endless list of wrongs inflicted on an outraged country.[36]

In the Federal military prison in Elmira, New York, Tennessean and Confederate Private Marcus B. Toney was still incarcerated, having refused to take an oath of allegiance to the Union after Lee's surrender. On the morning of 15 April 1865, the news ricocheted through the prison: "President Abraham Lincoln is dead—killed by a Rebel!" Toney heard a prisoner yell: "It's a good thing; old Abe oughta been kill'd long ago!" The guards rushed the man; trotted him to the commander's office. On orders they tied him up and hanged him by the thumbs. When he fainted, they cut him down and let him lie.

Toney had no sympathy for the fellow; he had jeopardized all their lives. Except for the guards who were stationed throughout the prison camp, Toney was sure the artillerymen would have turned on the prisoners with their guns. Toney remained quiet throughout the pandemonium.

Frightened speechless at the time his fellow prisoner rejoiced at the news of the assassination, Toney expressed his feelings about the assassination much later. As a returned prisoner-of-war, safely home again in Tennessee, he could think rationally and calmly about it all, and he wrote in his memoirs:

> I believe it was very unfortunate for the South that President Lincoln was assassinated. [If he had lived] I do not believe we would have had the . . . carpetbag rule and other trouble

---

[36]*Knoxville Whig,* 30 November 1864; 15 January 1865; 19 April 1865.

incident to the reconstruction policy adopted by the government. I believe President Lincoln would have said, "The South has made a mistake in secession, and you have not seceded because you cannot draw an imaginary line separating this country. We are Americans; let us be friends and brothers again." Of course we were uncertain as to our fate, and would have felt easier if President Lincoln rather than President Johnson was guiding the affairs of the nation, for the reason that we knew President Johnson hated and had no use for Rebels or, as he called them, 'secessionists.'[37]

Union Captain William H. Gay, whose company was encamped at Fort Negley overlooking Nashville, issued orders that a salute of fifty guns be fired to celebrate Grant's victory over Lee. He appointed Saturday, 15 April, for Nashville "to put on her brightest robes to shine beautiful in this hour of the nation's joy." Following his orders, at the appointed time, flag-bearers holding aloft the Stars and Stripes and the company colors, marched to take their places at the head of a parade. They were followed by a band, a fife and drum corps, the infantry, and artillery companies in all their splendor. Captain Gay mounted his horse to take his place at the head of his column of artillery. As he turned into College Street, a horseman galloped toward him exclaiming in a low, intense voice as he drew up beside him, "Have you heard the news?" As the horseman talked, Gay was speechless. He reeled in his saddle and uttered not a single word as he rode to the public square. There he met Governor Brownlow, who was seated in his carriage, his "strong, honest face showing the misery within." The glad acclaim of the morning soon subsided into "subdued mutterings of discontent. Joy turned to sorrow and hilarity to grief." The flags were dropped to half-mast; the day's celebratory program stopped; the loyal Nashville citizens returned to their houses to hang the crepe; other "well-known Southern citizens" remained safely hidden. As the day wore on, those

[37]Marcus B. Toney, *The Privations of a Private* (Nashville, Tennessee: Printed for the Author, 1905), 115-117.

who foolishly publicly declared their satisfaction at Lincoln's death had guns leveled at them. A few were shot.[38]

In Memphis, Federal soldiers shouldered their arms, left their barracks, and wandered the streets, looking for some show of satisfaction among the natives. For the most part, there was a pall of silence throughout the towns of Tennessee the rest of the day and into the night. Only the heavy footsteps of the blue-clad soldiers could be heard on the streets.

---

[38]William H. Gay, "Reminiscences of Abraham Lincoln, Quincy, and the Civil War," *Journal of Illinois History,* State Historical Society 7 (October 1914), 8:248-261; Wiley, "Billy Yank and Abraham Lincoln," *Abraham Lincoln Quarterly,* 6 (June 1950), 1:104.

Chapter 3

Reaction in
the Deep South

The war had begun in South Carolina when the Confederates fired upon Fort Sumter. Slavery had been most vital in the economy of the state, desire for secession strong, anti-Lincoln sentiment rife. This was true as well in other states of the deep South: Georgia, Alabama, Mississippi, Louisiana, Florida and Texas. But as the first state to secede from the Union, South Carolina was to General Sherman the place where treason began and where he swore it would end. With particular vengeance Sherman's armies devastated South Carolina. In the closing months of the war, and as Sherman's armies were sweeping the state toward Columbia, many Carolina slaveholders abandoned their homes, possessions, and former slaves. Benjamin Lawton Willingham, a Beaufort planter, was one of those who fled with his family to Georgia "to get out of the way of Sherman's army."[1]

To help the former slaves through the transition to freedom, the Federal government set up the Freedman's Aid Society. Esther Hill Hawks, a well-educated northerner with experience as both a doctor and a teacher, wanted to do what she could for the "poor demoralized and destitute black souls" in the South. She volunteered her services and was sent to Charleston.[2] Laura Towne was another northerner intensely stirred by the war news and the plight of the former slaves. The Sea Islands had become Union territory when she volunteered to "help take charge of the Negroes." She set sail for Port Royal in April

---

[1]Benjamin Lawton Willingham, *Family Bible,* entry regarding 10 January 1865. Bible now in the possession of Francis Fries Willingham, a great grandson.

[2]Esther Hill Hawks, *A Woman Doctor's Civil War*, ed. Gerald Schwarz (Columbia: University of South Carolina Press, 1984), 126-135.

1862. The planters had fled before the invaders, leaving their former slaves and their land behind. Towne went to St. Helena's, one of the Golden Isles on the South Carolina Coast, where she became one of several hundred workers whose aim was to create "some amount of order" and to stimulate "industry from the mass of eight or ten thousand contrabands." In what became known as the Port Royal Experiment, she worked as a manager-teacher in a little village on the wind-swept island. She labored there for forty years as a teacher of the freedpersons, where her "faith to the colored race was unswerving."[3]

Esther Hawks, unlike Laura Towne, did not serve on an island. She began her work in Charleston, where she selected a magnificent "abandoned" mansion on East Bay Street for her asylum for orphaned black children. A great many Charleston houses had been occupied by Union military families after Charleston surrendered. When the news of the evacuation of Richmond and the surrender of Lee's army reached the new occupants of the houses, it was greeted with wild rejoicing. The students in Esther's Normal School—running the school was another of her responsibilities—went about singing "Glory to God, our trials seem o'er!" The students reacted far differently when news of Lincoln's death reached them.

On St. Helena's Island, Laura Towne's African American pupils also showed great enthusiasm that Lee had surrendered and they were "free at last." Towne made her plans to go from the island to Charleston for the day-long victory celebration that the commanding officer of the Union forces was planning. Union officer Robert Anderson—now Brevet Major General, the same officer who had lowered the flag at Fort Sumter and folded it away four years before—would raise the flag again, this time in triumph. The famous anti-slavery champion and eloquent pulpiteer, the Reverend Henry Ward Beecher, was on his way from New York to deliver the main address. There would be other speeches by lesser personages; a parade along bunting-decorated streets,

---

[3]Laura M. Towne, *Letters and Diary of Laura M. Towne: Written from the Sea Islands of South Carolina*, ed. Rupert Sergent Holland (Cambridge: Riverside Press, 1912), i, xi, 150, 159.

gun salutes; and in the evening a grand gala. The editor of the *Charleston Courier* quickly pointed out that the ball was to take place in Middleton Mansion, which had been the rendezvous four years earlier of a "Brilliant assemblage of the beauty of Charleston." From the verandah the ladies had viewed the bombardment of the fort and the its eventual surrender to the rebels. Now the raising of the flag would be witnessed from the same verandah by "other beauties"—the wives and daughters of the Union military officers.[4]

Throngs watched the parade and flag-raising from vantage points along the waterfront. "Old Abe's" name received the greatest enthusiasm and everyone sprang to his feet to cheer whenever the "Great Emancipator" was mentioned by Beecher. Charleston was full of Yankee notables that day, including two judges, a member of Congress, and assorted citizenry, both black and white, military and non-military. Beecher was at his oratorical best, and the ball was a "sparkling collection of sparkling beauty." Longtime Charleston residents were conspicuous by their absence; the new occupants of their "deserted" houses were there in fine fettle. For the Unionists it was a most glorious day of celebration; for the rebels, a day of mute sadness.[5]

Lincoln died that same day. No public mention was made of it in Charleston during the festivities. If the Commanding Officer had received a dispatch from Secretary of War Stanton as had other commanders, he made no public announcement. Later, Edmund Ruffin noted the historical irony of the event. Ruffin had always considered Lincoln a "laughing stock", and when he heard the news of his death, he copied down in his diary every derogatory and abusive remark he could find about the dead president. Now Lincoln was dead; on the very day he drew his last breath, the United States flag was raised again over Sumter. But Ruffin's pleasure at Lincoln's death was far overshadowed by his devastation over the defeat of the Confederacy. When Lee was defeated, he prayed each night that he would not live to see the next day dawn. On 17 June he waited no longer for God to

---

[4]*Charleston Courier*, 21 April 1865.
[5]Ibid.

answer his prayers. He managed to place the muzzle of a loaded rifle in his mouth and twice pull the trigger with a forked stick. His last entry in his diary proclaimed "unmitigated hatred to Yankee rule—to all political, social & business connection with Yankees, & to the perfidious, malignant, & vile Yankee race."[6]

The steamer *Fulton* arrived at Hilton Head Island the Tuesday following Lincoln's death "with the sad intelligence of the assassination," and under the bold-faced type "IMPORTANT", the *Courier* reprinted the story taken from the New York papers.[7] Not until Henry Ward Beecher returned to his home in Brooklyn did he have the opportunity to preach a sermon honoring the slain President. On Easter Sunday he unleashed his full talents to the loyalists gathered in his home church, the Plymouth Congregational Church in Brooklyn. He consoled the grieving, praised the slain President, and propounded his conviction that the rebellion, the war, the assassination, all resulted from slavery, "which is a deadly poison to soul and body." The murderer Booth was "suckled and nursed in the slave system [and] was a logical outgrowth of its cruel and boistrous [sic] passions."[8]

Classes at Esther Hawks' school in Charleston had barely begun Wednesday morning when she received the news of the assassination. The school had been in operation only a few months, but already enrollment numbered six hundred black pupils. Of the teachers assigned to the classes, two were from New England, and there were nine white and five black South Carolinians. Several of the older girls who were in classes taught by the white Southern teachers came to Miss Hawks, weeping and asking to be taken out of their classes. Esther Hawks noted in her journal:

> I let them go home at the time—and must watch my teachers for any expression of disloyalty. The greatest gloom pervades

[6]Betty Mitchell, *Edmund Ruffin: A Biography* (Bloomingdale, Indiana: Indiana State University, 1981), 251-256.

[7]*Charleston Courier,* 20 and 22 April 1865.

[8]Carl Sandburg, *Abraham Lincoln: The War Years*, vol. 4 (New York: Harcourt Brace, 1939), 339.

the city. Every native is looked at suspiciously—and I have no doubt but the least expression of gratification at this national calamity will be dealt roughly with. Minute guns have been firing nearly ever since the news came, flags are at half mast. The colored people express their sorrow and sense of loss in many cases, with sobs and loud lamentations! No native whites are seen anywhere on the streets. When the children came to school they all wore little crape [sic] rosettes or bows, and in most of the school rooms an attempt to trim with mourning has been made, back of my desk there was hung a lovely wreath of roses tied with black crape [sic] . . . all done without any suggestions from us. There are constant complaints of teachers expressing sentement [sic] in hearing of the children and I have been obliged to dismiss one of them for speaking with disrespect of the murdered President. For me, I am beginning to be strong in the "fatalistic theory." His work was accomplished and he is removed. I will not doubt but God has other men and means to finish what is yet undone.[9]

Laura Towne and some of her charges from St. Helena's Island attended the great celebration in Charleston "on the very day the vile assassin was doing his work, or had accomplished it." She had never before seen such enthusiasm "by the freed people of Charleston—every time [Lincoln's] name was mentioned." When the news of his death reached St. Helena's Island, the blacks became inconsolable, not able to believe he was dead. In church on Easter Sunday, the black children prayed for Lincoln as if he were wounded but still alive. They said he was their Savior, that Christ had saved them from sin, and Lincoln had saved them from bondage.[10]

On another island, Hilton Head, a similar reaction among African Americans was recorded. A Northern teacher wrote to his family that

---

[9]Hawks, *A Woman Doctor's Civil War*. Diary entry, 22 April 1965, as quoted on 134.

[10]Towne, *Letters and Diary*, 150, 159

the death of Lincoln was an awful blow to the former slaves. In the aftermath of the assassination, African Americans expressed fear that their new Northern friends would desert them; that they would "Have to go North and Secesh [would] come back. We're going to be slaves again," they said.[11]

On the day designated for mourning in Charleston, the minister of the Methodist Episcopal Church spoke to a congregation of three thousand on the "inscrutability of God's ways" in the death of Lincoln. The Unitarian congregation of the city adopted a resolution of mourning and regret over the "appalling calamity." Henry Wilson Ravenel, a native South Carolinian, wrestled with his conscience before deciding to attend services for "humiliation and prayer for the death of Presdt. Lincoln [as proclaimed] by Presdt. Johnson." Ravenel considered the propriety of it, and concluded that the people should indeed attend. The doors of the church were opened, but no congregation gathered at the Presbyterian Church near Ravenal's home. He found only a few attendees at his Hampton Hall church, where he slipped into a pew and remained throughout the service. After the service, he wrote at length in his diary about his feelings that Southerners should not be expected to observe the day of mourning with the same fervor as those who admired the late President for all his acts toward "our Southern Confederacy." He then observed,

> [A]s it is enjoined upon us in holy writ to give due respect to the powers that be, I hold it as a duty in our new relations to show at least this outward respect to an order from the Chief Magistrate of the country.[12]

---

[11]Elizabeth Ware Pearson, ed., *Letters from Port Royal Written at the Time of the Civil War* (Boston: W.B. Clark Company, 1906), T. E. R. to C. P. N. St. Helena Island, 6 May 1865, as quoted, 310-311.

[12]*Charleston Courier*, 20 and 24 April 1865; Abbott, "Southern Reaction to the Assassination," *Abraham Lincoln Quarterly*, 4 (September, 1952), 3:123; *The Private Journal of Henry William Ravenel, 1859-1887*, ed. Arney Robinson Childs (Columbia: The University of South Carolina Press, 194), Entry for 1 June 1865, 241.

Eleanor H. Cohen, the daughter of Philip Melvin Cohen, a distinguished Jewish physician in Charleston, and a passionate supporter of the Confederacy, found little to mourn in Lincoln's demise. Her love of the South was equalled only by her love of B. M. Seixas, who served for a time as a soldier in the South Carolina Volunteers. During the last months of the war, Eleanor lived in Columbia, where she experienced "crushed hopes, wasted life, and fruitless exertion." She heard of the assassination after Columbia had fallen to Union troops. It made her blood boil to see "them" in the streets, Lincoln's assassination brought some feelings of relief to Eleanor. At last, she felt their worst enemy had been laid low. Then she heard that the Yankee Congress had a row, and that Andy Johnson was killed. "God grant so may all our foes perish!" she prayed.[13]

In Pendleton, South Carolina, Henry Gourdin was outraged by a meeting recently called in Charleston of "respectable, well-known and influential South Carolina gentlemen to express sorrow over Lincoln's assassination." To his dismay, these gentlemen and "people everywhere" were submitting to the will of the enemy in their midst. In the words of Gourdin "[T]hey yield[ed] their liberties to an inescapable necessity." If the proceedings of the meeting had been limited to the condemnation of assassination and murder, and "more especially to the assassination and murder of Lincoln, it would have been all very well. [B]ut expressions of sympathy and condolence with our oppressors in anything which concerns them come not well from our people." Sadly, the meeting was only another sign of the times, Gourdin felt; an indication that in their extremity, "Men seek protection first and liberty afterwards."[14]

Emma LeConte, who had unhappily witnessed the destruction of much of Columbia, now joyfully penned in her diary, "Hurrah! Old Abe Lincoln has been assassinated! It may be abstractly wrong to be so

---

[13]Jacob Rader Marcus, *Memoirs of American Jews*, 1775-1865, vol. 3 (Philadelphia: The Jewish Publishing Society of America, 1956), Diary of Eleanor M. Cohen, 21 and 22 April 1865, as quoted 357-358; 366-367.

[14]Gourdin-Young Papers, Special Collections, Robert W. Woodruff Library, Emory University. Henry Gourdin to Robert Gourdin, 22 May 1865.

jubilant, but I just can't help it. After all the heaviness and gloom . . . this blow to our enemies comes like a gleam of light. We have suffered 'til we feel savage." On second thought, however, Emma concluded that there really was no reason to exult. Lincoln's murder would make no change in the South's position; furthermore it would only infuriate the enemy. Still, she could not help but be glad that "our hated enemy has met the just reward of his life."

Emma discussed the news with family and friends, all of whom were in a tremor of excitement. Her own exhilaration finally subsided, and a few days later she more soberly assessed what now would be happening as a result of Lincoln's demise: "Andy Johnson will succeed him—the rail-splitter will be succeeded by the drunken ass. Such are the successors of Washington and Jefferson—such are to rule the South." On the following Sunday, subdued and pensive, she listened with rekindling hope to her minister's words that they "must not despair," that even if they were overcome, "[T]hey would not be conquered—the next generation would see the South *free* and independent."[15]

The reaction of Georgians and Alabamians to news of the assassination was similar in many respects to that of South Carolinians. A wide path through Georgia was smoldering; Atlanta, was cold ashes by the time of Lincoln's death. Eliza Frances Andrews's father, who had served in Atlanta as a Georgia legislator before the war, did his best to hold the state in the Union, but he "might as well have tried to tie the Northwest wind with a pocket handkerchief," Eliza concluded. Eliza hated to say it, but her father was "almost the only man in Georgia who stood out for the Union." After the war was under way, there were indeed relatively few in the deep South who remained staunch Unionists. For example, Eliza's father, although opposed to secession, did not object when his sons joined the Confederate army; and Eliza remained an adamant rebel.

---

[15]Emma LeConte Diary, 16-20 April 1865, LeConte Papers, Southern Historical Collection, University of North Carolina.

Eliza was hardly settled in her seat on the train pulling out of the Augusta station on her way to Washington, Georgia, when a man thrust his head in the car and shouted, "Lincoln has been assassinated!" Startled, Eliza thought it a jest, but when she became convinced of the truth of it, she decided it was a "terrible blow for the South," for it placed "that vulgar renegade Andy Johnson in power, and will give the Yankees an excuse for charging us with a crime which was in reality only the deed of an irresponsible madman."[16]

Atlanta ladies, under the direction of a Union officer on the staff of Colonel Beroth Eggleston, stitched together a Union flag, and when it was ready, the Fifth Iowa Band played the Star Spangled Banner as the flag was hoisted upon the public square in front of Eggleston's headquarters. There in the blackened city it floated at half mast in honor of President Lincoln, assassinated in Washington. A few weeks later the Federal authorities called a public meeting in Atlanta to give all the opportunity to express their "honest and loyal sentiments with an earnest determination to preserve our common country and its matchless institution." On this occasion a committee of five Atlanta citizens, duly appointed by Federal authorities, drew up a statement, part of which resolved

> That in the assassination of Abraham Lincoln we gaze upon a deed horrible and horrifying. We hold it up to universal execration, earnestly trusting that not only the immediate perpetrators of the crime, so infamous and revolting, but that all remotely concerned may receive condign punishment.

There was even an attempt to erect a monument in or near the city of Atlanta to the memory of Abraham Lincoln. Union authorities again appointed a committee, its report was adopted, a million-dollar fund-raising campaign approved; but the monument never materialized.[17]

---

[16]Eliza F. Andrews, *The Wartime Journal of a Georgia Girl, 1864-1865*, ed. Spencer B. King (Macon, Georgia: Ardivan Press, 1960), 172-176.

[17]Warren Putnam Reed, *History of Atlanta Georgia* (Syracuse, New York: D. Macon, Publishers, 1889), 211, 213, 243.

Augusta, Georgia remained almost unspoiled by Union forces when they entered the city. At war's end, sutlers, carpetbaggers, and assorted riffraff overran the city, but, incongruously, at the time of Lincoln's death, the 176-foot chimney of the largest gunpowder factory in the Confederacy rose unharmed against the Augusta sky. In some respects, the hearts and minds of Augustans had become less traumatized by the rapidly occurring events of the war than had the wits and judgment of other Georgians whose homes had been bespoiled. One contributing factor to Augustans' attitude may have been John R. Stockton, manager of the *Augusta Constitutionalist.* Said to have been peculiar and eccentric but of sound judgment and executive ability, Stockton not only served as commander of Augusta's Clinch Rifles Company, but he kept his pro-Confederate sheet in publication well into the final months of the war. After the war, Stockton had written: "Mr. Lincoln had, to a certain extent, won upon our people." In him, Stockton believed, the South would have found a "lenient judge and strong protector." Stockton thought Augustans "sorrowed all the more for [Lincoln] when he fell, cruelly murdered."[18]

New Yorker N. S. Morse purchased Augusta's *Chronicle and Sentinel* during the war, and upon Lincoln's death, he penned his evaluation of the President. Morse considered the slain president

[A] great soul, vast in judgments and keen in perception—richly endowed with statesmanlike qualities and hard common sense, an iron strength of will, an immutability of purpose, which rose above all difficulties and opposition; and above all, a large and true heart . . . without a taint of malice or vindictiveness.[19]

---

[18]Rabun Lee Brantley, *Georgia Journalism of the Civil War*, Contributions to Education of George Peabody College of Teachers, Number 58 (Nashville, TN, 1929), 19; E. Merton Coulter, *The South During Reconstruction, 1865-1877* (Baton Rouge: Louisiana State University Press, 1947), 27; *Augusta (Georgia) Constitutionalist*, 27 September 1865.

[19]*Augusta Chronicle and Sentinel*, 1 May 1865; Abbott, "Southern Reaction," Lincoln Quarterly, 7 (September 1952) 3:126.

Ella Gertrude (Clanton) Thomas, a graduate of Macon Female College, a literate and loquacious Augusta Confederate sympathizer, was an avid reader of both Stockton's pro-Confederate *Constitutionalist* and Morse's pro-Yankee *Chronicle and Sentinel*. Her attitude toward Lincoln modulated throughout the war years, and when she heard of the assassination, she felt that in her heart she could not approve Booth's act. She had no cause to love Lincoln; her "womanly sympathys [sic] went out to President Davis. Not to save my right arm would I betray him . . . and yet I was beginning to think him despotic." Ella considered the pro-Union editor of the *Chronicle* a contemptible scamp whom she wished someone would give a good cowhiding. She added: "He throws off the thin cloak he wore before and presumes to dictate to our citizens, telling those who are not pleased, 'the best thing to do is leave.' " Ella had no intention of leaving, but she was more intensely opposed to the North than at any period of the war. Now that the South had surrendered and Lincoln was dead, she concluded, "[W]e can count with certainty upon nothing."[20]

Lizzie Hardin was in Eatonton, Georgia, in April 1865. Very possibly because her wartime experiences began in southwest Virginia, shifted to Kentucky, Tennessee, and by the time of Lincoln's death to Middle Georgia, her attitude toward the assassination was uniquely her own. There is probably no comparable record to the diary of a gentlewoman who, like Lizzie, lived on both sides of the lines. When she went with her mother and sister to Eatonton, she stopped keeping her journal, feeling she had been exiled to a "provincial nowhere." She resumed her diary when the excitement and confusion of a world tumbling down engaged even the farthest reaches of the Confederacy. As Ella Thomas closely followed the two opposing Augusta newspapers, so Lizzie Hardin closely followed the editorial comments of whatever newspapers she could get her hands on in Eatonton. In the early days of April, she arrived at some conclusions about the general

---

[20]Ella Gertrude [Clanton] Thomas Diary, 1848-1889. Manuscript Department William R. Perkins Library, Duke University. Entries of 7 May 1865, typescript copy, 66-69.

condition of Confederate newspapers, which she entered in her diary of 10 April 1865;

> If when our cities are taken over our newspapers would only discontinue, we might reap some good from our disasters. A true and enlightened press is certainly the blessing to a country, but a *corrupt press owned by factious politicians* is the greatest curse, and when we enumerate all the forces against which we had to contend in order to gain our liberty, I think our press will not be among the least of them.

Lizzie read the account of the assassination in one of the late-arriving newspapers; she talked with friends who had seen Yankee papers containing the account, and, on 26 April, she had the good fortune to get hold of a paper, the Augusta *Constitutionalist*—the paper so greatly admired by Ella Thomas—which "through every trial has held out bravely for the South, her cause, and her President." From her study of the papers and conversations with friends and family about the crime, Lizzie concluded that the assassination was wrong, of course, but she sincerely admired the man or men who committed it. It was thrilling to Lizzie that Lincoln's assassin sprang upon the stage and cried, "Sic semper tyrannis! The South is avenged!" To one living in the South who had seen "the half-starved woman and children wandering amid the ashes of their once happy home," it seemed that the assassination was a wrong for which there were many excuses. "Well, poor creature," she wrote after she had absorbed the reports from various sources, "I sincerely hope [Lincoln] was better prepared for death than we think he was. But for the sake of my country, I cannot but feel glad that he is dead."[21]

Confederate Major Charles Seaton Henry Hardee safely delivered a box containing two million dollars of Confederate currency to Macon,

---

[21]Lizzie Hardin, *The Private War of Lizzie Hardin,* ed. G. Glenn Clift (Frankfort, Kentucky: The Kentucky Historical Society, 1965), ii, xiii, 22 (diary entry of 10 April 1865); 233-235 (Diary entries of 23 and 26 April 1865); Davis, *Image of Lincoln,* 99.

Georgia—practically worthless by the time it reached its destination. Hardee made the delivery to a safe repository in the nick of time; Union General James H. Wilson and his regiment of cavalry soon occupied Macon, but with scarcely more than a scuffle. Many Maconites fled before Wilson's forces, and Hardee proceeded swiftly and safely to the Parson plantation, a short distance south of Macon. There Hardee and a few other South Georgia Confederates received the news of Booth's crime at a store near the plantation. All but Hardee hurrahed and threw hats into the air.

"Why are you so silent, Major?" one asked. "I am silent because I do not think the assassination is a cause for rejoicing," he replied.

On the contrary I think it is the worst calamity that could happen to the Southern people at the particular time. Lincoln . . . was in perfect accord with his party, and was not as bitterly disposed towards the South as the majority of his party. . . . Now that he is dead and matters have passed into the hands of bitterest partisans and most unscrupulous politicians of his party, the South is likely to be looked upon as conquered country, and treated accordingly.[22]

Shortly before Christmas 1864, the editors of Savannah's two newspapers hastily abandoned their presses and joined a steady stream of rebel soldiers and civilians who moved silently into the fog on pontoon bridges across the Savannah River. They slipped away from Savannah, through the last gap not yet closed by Sherman's encircling army. As the fleeing citizens expected, Sherman and his forces occupied the city shortly thereafter. For whatever reasons he may have had, Sherman ordered that the city not be torched. An exuberant Sherman wired a telegram to Lincoln, giving a Christmas gift to his President: a relatively unspoiled jewel, Georgia's seaport city, Savannah. Upon seizing control of the city, Sherman set up temporary headquarters, and

---

[22]Martha Gallaudet Waring, ed., "Reminiscences of Charles Seton Henry Hardee," *Georgia Historical Quarterly*, 12 (September 1928), 265.

directed that "not more than two newspapers be published in Savannah," and their "Editors and Proprietors [be] held to the strictest accountability and will be punished in person and property for any libelous publication. . . ." The day after Christmas the order was issued, and from then until well into the month of April 1865, the two newspapers, with new names, under new loyalist editors, maintained an editorial policy that brought no rebuke from the military. The first issues of the Savannah *Daily Loyal Georgian* left no doubt as to the paper's loyalties. The new masthead read: "The Union, It Must and Shall Be Preserved."[23]

When Sherman left the city for his push through South Carolina, he left Savannah in charge of a soldier experienced in public administration, Union General J. W. Geary, who had in the past been Mayor of San Francisco. The two newspapers continued to abide by the designated rules and policies set forth by Sherman. When a group of distinguished New York business leaders visited Savannah, the editors filled their columns with praise of the city, and expounded on the "good feelings between soldiers and civilians." But the true sentiments of the residents came through when the editor of the *Savannah Republican* reluctantly and with embarrassment reported that the proprietors of the Exchange, Savannah's oldest building, where presumably meetings were held with the visitors, "refused to fly the American flag" on Washington's birthday.[24]

After Lee's surrender at Appomattox, the headlines of the *Savannah Herald* declared it "The Most Glorious News of the War," and predicted that the Confederacy "will speedily be but a dark shadow of the past." Mary Capp was startled by this and other pro-Union stories. But to Mary what was even worse was that the *Herald*, the front page of which was typeset to resemble a monument, was dedicated to Lincoln's memory.[25]

---

[23]John E. Talmadge, "Savannah's Yankee Newspapers," *Georgia Review* 12 (Spring 1958) 66-73.

[24]Ibid., 72.

[25]Alexander A. Lawrence, *A Present for Mr. Lincoln: The Story of Savannah From Secession to Sherman* (Macon, GA: The Ardivan Press, 1961), 242; Aaron Wilbur

By the time of Lincoln's death, a loyalist civilian, R. D. Arnold, was serving as mayor of Savannah. Mayor Arnold called a meeting of the citizens "to give expression to their sentiments in relation to the assassination of President Lincoln." So large an assemblage gathered at the Exchange Building for the purpose that the meeting was adjoined to tree-lined Johnson Square. There the Mayor said, "Your immense assemblage is a sufficient guarantee that you comprehend the awfulness of the crime, socially, morally, and politically, and that you wish to set upon it the seal of your emphatic condemnation." The mayor appointed a committee to draft a "suitable resolution" expressive of the sense of the meeting. The committee's seven-point statement expressed "deepest pain and sorrow," for events that "even if they had occurred in the providence of God without human agency we would deplore, but we are especially and profoundly grieved at the manner of their occurrence."[26]

The resolution was duly signed, approved, and forwarded to the National Grand Council in Washington, D.C., where it was included in a special five-hundred-copy, leather-bound, gilt-edged official book of expressions of condolence and sympathy on the events of Lincoln's assassination. Expressions from numerous cities in the North, foreign governments, famous personages, special societies and organizations throughout the world made up the thick volume published in Washington by the Government Printing Office in 1867. Expressions from three Southern cities were included: New Orleans, Huntsville, Alabama, and Savannah, all prepared under the direction of the military commanders in the cities.[27]

Papers, Manuscript Department, William R. Perkins Library, Duke University, Mary E. Copp to her husband, 19 April 1865; Rabun L. Brantley, *Georgia Journalism*, 74.

[26]*The Assassination of Abraham Lincoln Late President of the United States of America, and the Attempted Assassination of Frederick H. Seward, Assistant Secretary on the Evening of the 14th of April, 1865. Expressions of Condolence and Sympathy Inspired by these Events* (Washington: Government Printing Office, 1867). Expressions from Savannah, Georgia, 917-919.

[27]See *Expressions of Condolence*, from Huntsville, Alabama, 858-859; from New Orleans, Louisiana, 898-899.

William Starr Basinger, a member of the Savannah Volunteer Guards, quietly recorded his personal feelings about the atrocity:

Lincoln was not a martyr for, as much as we may object to and condemn assassination, he committed a monstrous crime in making war upon us, and his tragic death was no more than just punishment for the crime.[28]

Charles Colcock Jones, Jr., throughout his adult life, faithfully carried on a spirited correspondence with his parents whenever he was separated from them for extended periods of time. Charles's letters to them most often reached his parents at one of the family's three plantations in Liberty County, Georgia, where the Reverend Jones, a Presbyterian minister, devoted himself to "the great work of his life," the evangelization of the slaves. In the fall of 1860, at age twenty-nine, Charles Jr. became Mayor of the city of Savannah. When Georgia seceded from the Union, Mayor Jones left his post to enlist in the First Regiment, Georgia Artillery. Still later in the war he became Chief of Artillery for the Military District of Georgia. Throughout the remainder of the war in his letters to his parents, Jones freely expressed his opinions of Lincoln and of events as they occurred. The flow of his letters to his mother slowed considerably by December 1864, when he was busily engaged as chief of artillery in Savannah. In February 1865, his mother, now a widow, wrote her sister about her deep concerns for her son. Other members of the large Jones clan kept their aged parent informed of personal and war news. Caroline S. Jones expressed her own sentiments and probably those of most other family members as well when she wrote Charles's mother in late April:

We are almost paralyzed here by the rapid succession of strange and melancholy incidents that have marked the last few

---

[28]Alexander A. Lawrence, *The Story of Savannah*, as quoted from the *Savannah Republican*, 19-23 April 1865, 242-243; William Starr Basinger, "The Savannah Volunteer Guards, 1852-1882," Manuscript Collection, University of Georgia, Athens.

weeks—the sudden collapse of our tried and trusted General Lee and his army, about which, sad as it is, I feel no mortification, for I know he did all that mortal man could do; then the rumors of peace, so different from the rapturous delight of a conquered peace we all looked forward to; then the righteous retribution upon Lincoln. One sweet drop among so much that is painful is that he at least cannot raise his howl of diabolical triumph over us."[29]

Such a sound of ringing bells as he had never heard before reverberated from the city of Sandusky, Ohio, across the water, and filled the barracks of the prison on Johnson's Island. Lieutenant-Colonel John W. Inzer of Asheville, Alabama, imprisoned with other captured rebel soldiers, rushed with fellow prisoners to the nearest vantage points to watch the little steamer, its own bells clanging, slip into the landing dock. Shortly, from atop the prison walls a Federal sentinel shouted, "Abraham Lincoln's dead! Assassinated!" In the prison yard, one prisoner cursed and shouted that Lincoln was in hell and he was glad of it. Cheer after cheer went up, punctuated by shouts and oaths. The excitement scarcely abated as Federal soldiers with guns in hand and bayonets fixed encircled the prisoners. Block houses where the artillery was kept were thrown open, and guns were charged and leveled at the prisoners.

From within his barracks, Inzer watched silently. "All this seemed to have no effect on the excited crowd," he recounted later:

The Confederates felt that all they had so often risked their lives for, [the] cause which was so near and dear to every true Confederate, [was] now almost departed. [They] had but little, if anything to lose, as life was not worth caring for and nothing

[29]Myers, ed., *Children of Pride*, Charles Colcock Jones, Jr., biography, 1568; Mrs. Mary Jones to Mrs. Susan M. Cumming, Montevideo, 11 February 1865, 1250; Mrs. Caroline S. Jones to Mrs. Mary Jones, Augusta, Georgia, 20 April 1865, 1267-1268; 1568.

was left them worth caring for. . . . The conclusion and judgment of a large majority of the prisoners was that it was well for them and their cause and for the South that Lincoln was no more President of the United States; notwithstanding, at the same time, they had a great horror of Andrew Johnson. Still others thought that the killing of Lincoln and the promotion of Johnson to the Presidency would prove a calamity to the South.

Although he deplored Booth's act as cowardly and villainous, Inzer was quite relieved at Lincoln's death. He explained that but for Booth's act more than 300,000 men, including Inzer himself and his fellow prisoners from Alabama, would have been perjured. They had all solemnly sworn that they would *never* live under a government presided over by Abraham Lincoln. Most of them would have been compelled to do so but for the act of Booth in the assassination of Lincoln.[30]

Another Alabama prisoner of war, Captain Robert E. Park, in his bed in the Fort Delaware Prison Hospital, who referred to his company as the "Macon [County, Alabama] Confederates," had daily access to "rabid, black Republican papers" while he and other wounded rebel prisoners lived under the watchful eyes of "seemingly kind" Yankee guards. Park was the only officer in his ward who managed to buy a paper on the morning of 15 April. A nurse brought him a copy of the *Inquirer* hurriedly and stealthily at a late hour. The first words of the first column startled Park: "Assassination of President Lincoln, John Wilkes Booth the Murderer." He called out to his hospital comrades, who left their bunks and crowded around him. As Park read the story, one man declared he would gladly divide his last crust of bread with Booth if he ever met him. Shortly, the prison commander ordered every man who could walk to go from the hospital ward to the Barracks. "[H]e evidently regards us as accomplices of Wilkes Booth," Park

---

[30]John W. Inzer, "How the News of the Assassination of President Lincoln was Received by confederate Prisoners on Johnson's Island in April 1865," *Gulf States Historical Magazine*, 1 (July 1902 to May 1903) 194-198.

observed. The commander also ordered his guards to fire upon any rebel who manifested pleasure at the news. Careful not to express his feelings openly in the Fort Delaware Prison environment, Park confided to his diary that he looked upon Lincoln as a tyrant and an inveterate enemy of the South. He could shed no tears for him, he wrote, but he did "deprecate the cruel manner of his taking off." Park assessed the reactions of his fellow prisoners. A large majority of them regretted Lincoln's death, he believed. "[I]n the wonderful charity which buries all quarrels in the grave [they no longer] regarded the dead President . . . as an enemy, for, with the noble generosity native to Southern character, all resentment was hidden in his death."[31]

Captain Edward Crenshaw, a native of Butler County, Alabama with his unit in Virginia, was convinced the war was almost over when "reliable information" came to his unit that President Lincoln had been killed. Crenshaw had been sick and feverish for days, hardly able to keep going, spending much of his flagging energies in planning with another rebel captain, also sick, how they would stay together until they got well and try to go through to Alabama together if the Confederate Government had "broken up." Not much interested in anything but getting well and getting home to Alabama, Crenshaw did, however, express regret at Lincoln's death, feeling that it was "unfortunate that it should have happened at this particular time." Wounded, sad and sick, he wrote,

So after four years of bloodshed and sacrifice we are compelled to give up our high aspirations for a great and glorious Southern Confederacy, and will have to come back into the old Union. . . . We await coming events with anxious hearts.[32]

---

[31]Robert E. Park, "Diary of Robert E. Park, Twelfth Alabama Regiment," *Southern Historical Society Papers* 3 (June 1877) 6:245-246, 249, 253-254; diary entries of 5-10 April 1865, 30 April-18 May 1965.

[32]Edward Crenshaw, "Diary of Captain Edward Crenshaw of the Confederate States Army," *Alabama Historical Quarterly* 2 (Winter 1940) 4:465-471, entries of 8-19 April 1865.

Another Alabamian, John Johnston, at the time he was released from his regiment after Lee's surrender in Virginia, had a "little ole leather-back memorandum book" in which he "kept a very poor sort of diary." He often pulled his little book from his frayed pocket to record his thoughts. One day, in tiny, cramped handwriting he recorded: "There is great enthusiasm in camp. Lincoln has undoubtedly been assassinated. God grant that this may not prove a myth!" It was a happy day for Johnston when he could note, "Our regiment stacked their arms this morning, racking and saddling up, & in the night, anxious thoughts of home."[33]

By the time of Lincoln's assassination, Huntsville, Alabama, had long been under Union control. Since 11 April 1862, when General Ormsby M. Mitchell moved into the town and quartered his officers there, the town became a communications center and Union headquarters for the Northern Alabama District. Except for ten months in 1862 and 1863, Huntsville remained occupied or under passive siege until the end of the war. Union officers who administered the city government were often hard-put to supplant the stern and austere home guard that Huntsville's formidable womenfolk maintained. Left to carry on at home without their men who took up arms for the Confederacy, the ladies met each Yankee indignity with poise and chilly reserve. Their unofficial authority and influence among the town folk went far deeper than the authority of the Yankees in official charge of the city.[34]

One of the redoubtable ladies of influence in the town was Mary Cook Chadick, wife of the Reverend William D. Chadick, who had taken up Bible and cross to serve as Chaplain of the Fourth Alabama Regiment on the first day of the Union "takeover." With firm resolve and forthrightness, Mary and a group of ladies confronted General Mitchell to secure permission to minister to the sick and attend the wounded prisoners in the boxcars at the depot. On many occasions,

---

[33]John Johnston Papers, "Diary, Civil War Reminiscences," Southern Historical Collection, University of North Carolina. Entries for April 1865 and 8 May 1865.

[34]Elise Hopkins Stephens, *Historic Huntsville: A City of New Beginnings* (Woodbine Hills, California: Winsor Publications, 1984), 50-54.

Mary served as self-appointed liaison for the military and the townspeople.[35] On one of her resolute trips to the Provost Marshal's office—this one to have three letters approved for mailing—the marshal, while examining the letters, remarked to Mrs. Chadick:

> We have just got news that I fear will be worse for you Southern people than anything that has yet happened. President Lincoln was shot last night, at the theatre in Washington, and died this morning.

Mary did not record her response to the marshal, but in the privacy of her home, she wrote that she was exceedingly shocked and felt in her heart that "it must be bad news for the South, if Andrew Johnson was to succeed him."

The day following Lincoln's death, General Gordon Grainger, Commander of the North Alabama District, issued orders that "all persons exalting in the death of President Lincoln shall be summarily punished." Sentries observed a group of young ladies and an elderly gentleman laughing and talking on a front porch. They searched the house, removed some of the furniture, and threatened to burn the dwelling. Next day, Ella Scruggs and Edmonia Toney were arrested and taken to the courthouse on the charge of rejoicing at the news. The officer-in-charge read them a stern lecture before dismissing them.[36]

Clement C. Clay, who had represented Alabama in both the United States and Confederate Senates, was one of many officials who fled after Richmond fell. In fact, Clay was with Davis on part of the "sad journey through the Carolinas." Although Clay's wife, Virginia, confessed to "a confused memory" regarding the evacuation of Richmond and the murder of Lincoln, she recorded her vivid

---

[35]Ibid., 53-54.

[36]Mary [Cook] Chadick, "Civil War Days in Huntsville," *Alabama Historical Quarterly,* 9 (Summer 1947) 2:319-333, diary entries for 15-18 April 1865.

recollection of her husband's reaction to the news of the assassination: "A kind of horror seized my husband when he realised the truth of the reports that reached us of the tragedy. At first he refused to credit them. 'It's a canard!' he said; but when, at last he could no longer doubt, he exclaimed, 'God help us! If that be true, it is the worst blow that yet has been struck at the South!' " Shortly after the assassination, Clay was arrested for conspiring with Jefferson Davis to kill Lincoln. Like Davis, Clay protested his innocence. An honest, forthright man, he fully expected, as had Davis, to clear his name and be promptly released. Instead, he languished in prison at Fortress Monroe for more than a year.[37]

Captain William H. Stewart, a Union officer from Illinois, was near Montgomery, Alabama, with his unit when Lincoln died. Stewart thought Montgomery and the Alabama countryside "beautiful and rich." But the citizens were "altogether another matter. They were a lot of proud, arrogant fools. Lincoln's death was almost a universal wish with them. They may look for a fearful retribution in bloody penalty. They will be handled with ungloved hands." "Look out!" he warned.[38]

In their reactions to the assassination, many Alabamians were, for the most part, glad Lincoln was gone. There was another group, however, who seemed relatively unaffected, who remained uncaring one way or the other whether Lincoln still held his post in Washington. William Cooper, still on his plantation near Tuscaloosa when Lincoln died, expressed what seemed to be the general reaction of the minority of Alabamians who were removed from active involvement in the day-by-day events and exigencies of the war. Cooper kept a small journal in which he noted daily events.

Many days after the assassination, when Cooper finally heard of Lincoln's death, he depicted in his journal the President's coffin resting upon a fine table draped with black gauze caught by a rosette. Beneath

---

[37]Ada Sterling, *A Belle of the Fifties, Memoirs of Mrs. [Virginia] Clay [Clopton] of Alabama, Covering Social and Political Life in Washington and the South, 1854-1866* (London: Wm. Heinemann, 1905), 241-245; Neely, *Lincoln Encyclopedia*, 311-312.

[38]William H. Stewart Diary, diary entry of 27 April 1865, Southern Historical Collection, University of North Carolina.

Lincoln's coffin and one for Seward ("W. H. Seward yet lives," he noted), he wrote the following words:

> Abram Lincoln was shot in the head on the 14 of April 1865 in Ford's Theatre in Washington City about 11 o'clock p.m. & died 15 April 1865 about 7 1/2 a.m. . . . J. Wilkes Booth charged with murder. . . . I think [Booth] was evidently crazy & at least a monomaniac on the subject of killing A. Lincoln and his death was a misfortune to the south particularly at this crisis—he was but the leader of a people & on his death the people would necessarily take another leader—this is not the age nor kind of goverment [sic] when the death of leaders affect much for the people rule & they are the goverment.[39]

Secretary of War Stanton's official announcement of the assassination floated down the Mississippi River on the *Steamboat Sultana*. Not until the word reached Baton Rouge at 12:30 p.m. on 19 April was the news hung upon the wire and sent to New Orleans. In the *New Orleans Daily Picayune* the words appeared: "Abraham Lincoln Assassinated April 14! Shot down at the supreme moment of his career, when Washington and all the North were celebrating Lee's surrender to Grant on 9 April. . . ." The *New Orleans Black Republican* denounced the murder as "an atrocity incomparable in human history." The black editor of the *New Orleans Tribune*, despite his previous criticisms of Lincoln's moderation, said simply: "Brethren we are mourning for a benefactor of our race. . . . Lincoln and John Brown are two martyrs, whose memories will live united in our bosoms." The night the news broke, Anthony P. Dostie and the radical leader Thomas J. Durant, spoke from a balcony of Dostie's office to free blacks assembled below.

---

[39]Thomas McAdory Owen, *History of Alabama and Dictionary of Alabama Biography* (Spartanburg, South Carolina: The Reprint Company, 1895) III:399; Diary of William Cooper, Manuscripts, Alabama State Archives, Montgomery, entries for 14 April 1865 (facing "Moon Phases" for March, 1865), another entry dated 14 April 1865 as well as entries for 31 January 1865; 2, 3, and 17 April 1865; 6, 7, and 15 May 1865; 11 June 1865; 10 July 1865.

They called for black suffrage and a new state election. Afterwards, Durant returned to his home on Canal Street where a bust of Lincoln was prominently displayed in the hallway. He began to think through what had occurred and what Africans should do to meet this new challenge now that their benefactor was murdered.[40]

All New Orleans newspapers gave detailed accounts of the assassination and advice to the readers about how they should behave and react to the news. They printed orders from the commanding general and plans for observing the day of mourning. New Orleanians observed the day according to directions. In common with other Southern cities under martial law, observance of the day in New Orleans included tolling bells, black-draped flags at half mast, crepe hung on all public buildings, business suspended, a public meeting attended by crowds of the city's most influential citizens, who listened to eulogies and delighted to do Lincoln honor. All the news reports emphasized the horror and grief that "ran rife through the streets." The sentiments of "every citizen present, it matters not what his occupation or calling, were of the most unfeigned regret at the atrocity of the crime."[41]

As in other Union-occupied cities—Savannah and Huntsville—resolutions were drawn up in New Orleans after the public days of mourning. The resolution for New Orleans, properly approved and signed, was also sent to Washington to be included in the gilt-edged book of condolences from throughout the nation and the world.[42]

Union Lieutenant Colonel Henry Clay Warmoth believed that in the months preceding Lincoln's death, cordial, even affectionate relations had sprung up between the citizens and the Union soldiers assigned to the city. Warmoth was away on special assignment on the

---

[40]Peyton McCrary, *Abraham Lincoln and Reconstruction, The Louisiana Experiment* (Princeton, New Jersey: Princeton University Press, 1978), 309; *(New Orleans) Times,* 20, 22, and 23 April 1865; *(New Orleans) Black Republican,* 22 April 1865; *(New Orleans) Tribune,* 22 April 1865; *(New Orleans) Daily Picayune,* 19 April 1865.

[41]*(New Orleans) Weekly Times,* 22 April 1865; *Picayune,* 19 and 20 April 1865; *Tribune,* 20 April 1865; *Black Republican,* 22 April 1865.

[42]*Expressions of Condolence.* From New Orleans, 898-899.

day of Lincoln's death. He served as an official escort for the body, accompanying Lincoln's funeral cortege from Washington as far as New York. Soon thereafter, Warmoth returned to New Orleans where he found that formerly cordial relations between the two factions had precipitously cooled. The atmosphere was charged with rumors and individual acts that "keep the people in a state of the wildest suspicion and excitement," excitement and fears fueled by the assassination.

Warmoth observed no "unfeigned mourning" among the white rebels, but he did observe that "more than ten thousand blacks paraded the city streets." What was far more ominous, Warmoth notes, was that the black-controlled New Orleans *Tribune* was raising the hopes of fellow blacks by suggesting that Louisiana might become a "Negro State," thereby contributing to hysterical reactions by ex-rebels. Warmoth remained in Louisiana after Lincoln's death and his discharge from the Union army. In 1868, as Governor of Louisiana, he still found the "whole South in a state of turmoil," a turmoil seemingly triggered by Lincoln's assassination and the editorial policy of the *Tribune*.[43]

Charlotte, a former slave, worked in New Orleans for her white Unionist friend, Mrs. William P. Rucker. Charlotte was working there the day the news arrived in the Rucker household. Deeply distressed, Charlotte wailed, "The colored people have lost their best friend on earth." In a burst of grief and zeal, she declared that she would give five dollars of her wages—a fortune to an ex-slave—toward erecting a monument to Lincoln's memory. The Ruckers, touched by the offer, directed the gift toward a local clergyman, C. D. Battelle, who "cheerfully did what he could to promote so noble an object." A total of $16,242.00 was raised, every dollar of which came from former slaves.[44]

Sarah Morgan Dawson, a native of New Orleans, was a firm Confederate sympathizer who violently detested the first Union general put in charge of the city, Benjamin F. ("that Beast") Butler." Her

---

[43]Henry Clay Warmoth, *War, Politics, and Reconstruction* (New York: The Macmillan Company, 1930), viii, ix, 28, 31-33, 49.

[44]Benjamin Quarles, *Lincoln and the Negro* (New York: Oxford University Press, 1962), 5, 244-246.

patriotism for the Confederacy, however, was second to her strong yearning for peace. An intelligent, thoughtful young lady, she evaluated events in terms of the welfare of the nation, and her diary portrays a woman who calmly refused to accede to the blind intolerance and sectional hatred of many of her New Orleans neighbors. Everybody but Sarah cried when tidings of Lee's surrender reached the friends. Sarah was "satisfied that God would save us, even though all should apparently be lost." She lost her calm when her brother read the newspaper at breakfast one morning, "Lincoln Assassinated." "This is murder!" she cried. "God have mercy on those who did it!" Sarah abhorred the deed, not only because she felt that the enemy "would have apotheosized any man who had crucified Jeff Davis, "but because she found that his blood "would be visited on our nation." As Sarah wrote in her diary, she noticed that across the way from her home a large building, undoubtedly inhabited by Union officers, was being draped in black; black streamers hung from the balcony, which, Sarah was sure, would have been banners if Jefferson Davis had been killed. Shortly, according to Sarah, the whole town assumed a funerary demeanor; men who hated Lincoln with all their souls, under terror of confiscation and imprisonment that they understood as the alternative, hastily tied black crepe from every possible doorknob and point, "to save their homes." And Sarah's friends, with bitter tears in their eyes, tears that had nothing to do with pity and sorrow for Lincoln's death, festooned their homes with "this vile, vile old crape [sic]!"[45]

Sarah and her friends in their frantic hanging-on-the-crepe to save themselves and their homes were representative of pro-Confederate Louisianians who strenuously attempted to disassociate themselves and the South as a whole from the assassination. Ambivalent or even joyful though their feelings may have been, they openly and repeatedly expressed sorrow at his death.

---

[45]Sarah Morgan Dawson, *A Confederate Girl's Diary*, Edited with a foreword and notes by James I. Robertson, Jr. (Bloomington: Indiana University Press, 1960), xiii-xvii; Sarah Morgan Dawson, *A Confederate Girl's Diary*, with an introduction by Warrington Dawson (Boston: Houghton Mifflin, 1913), 46-438.

E. Earl was a member of a Northern family who had earlier moved to Walton Plantation in the Louisiana low country. Earl felt that there was good reason for rebels to fear retaliation for the assassination. He believed the murder was a mad act, one for which ex-Confederates "will bitterly repent." He prayed for President Johnson to have wisdom to perform the difficult task of reconstruction that lay ahead. William J. Minor, another Unionist plantation owner, sold his wares in New Orleans, the great port of the sugar land. Minor felt that Lincoln had been the ablest and most conservative man in Washington and his death was a loss to the whole country. He felt sure that the South "had a right to expect better terms of peace from [Lincoln] than from anyone else likely to come into power."[46]

While Unionist planters on Louisiana lands—Earl and Minor among them—deeply lamented Lincoln's death, staunch rebel plantation owners had entirely different reactions to the act. Louisiana planter Louis A. Bringler, still serving as commander of the Confederate 7th Louisiana Regiment in April 1865, had undergone "great and sad disasters" that had been showered upon him by the enemy. But one day, one piece of "good news" cheered him up considerably when he received it: "The death of the tyrant old Abe."[47]

The state of Mississippi, including Natchez and the key city of Vicksburg, went along with the military-directed mourning procedures that were being followed throughout enemy-occupied areas of the deep South. Richard Alexander Hall was officer-of-the-day in Natchez when the news came that "made the Blood run cold." When his commanding general was told of the dispatch announcing Lincoln's death, he swore,

---

[46]R. L. Reid, "Louisiana and Lincoln's Assassination: Reactions in a Southern State," *Southern Historian* 6 (Spring 1986) 22:21-27; Bell I. Wiley, "Billy Yank and Abraham Lincoln," *Abraham Lincoln Quarterly* 7 (June 1950) 2:119: New York *Times,* April 27, 1865; Dobbins Papers, Special Collection, University of Kentucky Libraries, Lexington, KY., E. Earl to son, 24 May 1865; Charles P. Roland, *Louisiana Sugar Plantations During the American Civil War* (Leiden: E. J. Brill Publisher, 1959), 8, 127-128.

[47]Louis A. Bringler and Family Papers, Department of Archives and Manuscripts, Louisiana State University, Baton Rouge, Louisiana. Louis A. Bringler to wife, 23 April 1865.

"Hell's not hot enough for the villains." Then he issued orders that Hall carried out, to have black crepe tied on the sword hilts of the officers and black bands on their arms.[48] It was in Natchez that one Catholic Bishop—a resolute Confederate—expressed what he explained was the attitude of the Catholic Church toward the crime of Lincoln's murder. To Bishop William Henry Elder, Lincoln's murder was more than an outrage against mankind, it was also "a dishonor to Almighty God, and was certain to bring punishment upon the entire people of the country." Elder forthwith gathered the faithful together at the Catholic Church in Natchez and delivered a stirring pastoral message. Assembling his parishioners as he did, Elder explained, was a "holy practice of the Church when extraordinary crimes have been committed," to exhibit "extraordinary marks of reverence and affection for their outraged Father . . . with resolutions to serve Him more fervently than ever."[49]

To the astonishment and shock of most Americans, other "staunch Catholics" had an entirely different view of the assassination. As Victor Searcher explained: "The powerful political force of orthodox Christianity was aligned *against* Lincoln and the Union," in the struggle for human freedom and dignity. He further noted:

> To indoctrinated consciences, the murder of Lincoln for religious purposes [was] justified by the theory of ruling by 'divine right' [that was] the self-serving theory that God appoints the rulers of men.[50]

A formal resolution on the death of President Lincoln was adopted and signed by the officers of the army and navy and selected citizens of

---

[48]Letter, Richard Alexander Hall to Mother and Father, 21 April 1865. Christian Koch and Family Papers (1864-1867), Department of Archives and Manuscripts, Louisiana State University, Baton Rouge, LA.

[49]Willard E. Wight, ed. "The Bishop of Natchez on the Death of Lincoln," *Lincoln Herald* 58 (Fall 1956), 13-14.

[50]Victor Searcher, *Lincoln Today: An Introduction to Modern Lincolniana* (New York: Thomas Yoseloff, 1965), 159, as quoted.

Natchez who were known to be loyal Unionists. The resolution, carefully worded, approved, and signed by Brigadier General J. W. Davidson, was published by the *Natchez Courier* printing office. The document proclaimed that the citizens of Natchez "sorrowfully recognized the public calamity and impious crime, which deprived the nation of its Chief Magistrate" for which was demanded

> a punishment as just and severe as the assault was base and cowardly to be visited not only upon the one who accomplished the foul deed, but against all who conspire against the life of the nation."

The General directed that the resolution be widely distributed among all the citizens.[51]

In April 1865 almost 4,000 freedpersons remained in the refugee camps along the Mississippi River. The camps were the responsibility of only a handful of "missionaries and teachers," together with a scattering of civilians in the medical service, a few enlisted men and a Union officer. The contingent of caretakers and their charges briefly celebrated Lee's surrender, but the surrender of the Confederate general seemed irrelevant to those in the camp. A week later, however, the reaction to Lincoln's death was immediate and strong. Union soldier Samuel D. Barnes recorded, "All the colored people have crape [sic] black strung or mourning of some kind for as their Uncle Sam, Massa Lincoln is dead."[52]

William P. Chambers had decided days before when he heard that Lee had surrendered to Grant, that it was useless for him and his disorganized rebel soldiers near Meridian to contend longer with the

---

[51]"Resolutions Adopted at a Meeting of the Officers of the Army and Navy and the Citizens of Natchez, on the Death of the President of the United States," *Natchez (Mississippi) Courier* pamphlet, 19 April 1865. Rare Books and Special Collections Division, The Library of Congress, Washington, D.C.

[52]James T. Currie, *Enclave: Vicksburg and her Plantations, 1863-1870* (Jackson, Mississippi: University Press of Mississippi, 1980), 105, as quoted from Barnes Diary, 23 April 1865.

odds against them. When a train chugged slowly by that night, he swung aboard, arriving at Meridian at daylight. All the members of Chamber's regiment who had escaped capture, he found in Meridian. They were circulating the sensational news of the assassination. The reports were well authenticated, Chambers believed, and with many misgivings he concluded that the war would be prosecuted more barbarously than ever, now that Lincoln was dead, for "I have a poor opinion of the moderation of such a man as Andrew Johnson."[53]

In 1862-1863 Union troops captured four of Florida's coastal cities—Fernandino, Jacksonville, St. Augustine, and Tampa. But it was not until May 1865—more than a month after Lee's surrender and Lincoln's death—that Tallahassee was occupied and residents ran onto the streets to watch quietly as Federal officers entered the city and were very properly received by city representatives. For the most part, Confederate Floridians reacted to the assassination with neither joy nor sorrow. With subdued emotions they adjusted to whatever was required of them in observing days of mourning. By the time of Lincoln's death many had lost their will to fight. Although the act of murder was condemned, the demise of the President did not arouse much emotion among the citizens or rekindle any will to continue the struggle.[54]

A prominent lawyer, Edward McCrady L'Engle, who had served as captain with Florida troops in Virginia, had a unique reaction to the death of Lincoln. L'Engle was back home in Florida when he wrote to his brother on 29 April 1865, expressing certainty that Lincoln's assassination and the consequent "grasp after the fallen scepter" would benefit the South and secure the Confederacy a "separate nationality."[55]

---

[53]William P. Chambers, *My Journal* (Jackson, Mississippi: Mississippi Historical Society, 1925), vol. 5, Centenary Series, 375-376, entry of 17 April 1865.

[54]John E. Johns, *Florida During the Civil War* (Gainesville: University of Florida Press, 1963), 208-209.

[55]Letter, Edward McCrady L'Engle to brother Francis, 29 April 1865. Edward McCrary L'Engle Papers, Southern Historical Collection, University of North Carolina, Chapel Hill.

This opinion was not shared by Union officer Peter Kitts who was stationed at Fort Jefferson in South Florida. When the soldiers within the fort heard that Lee had surrendered, a quickly assembled group who called themselves "Webb's Minstrels" struck up several lively tunes, and sixteen hundred pounds of powder fed the fort's guns thatbegan to fire in joyful salute. Kitts rejoiced over Lee's surrender with the rest of the troops at the fort, but only a few days later the "awful and horrid" news of the murder saddened all the men there—"just at the time when victory was crowning our armies," Kitts explained. Some of the Union soldiers tackled the rebel prisoners at the fort—there were fifteen or twenty who had been pilots for blockade runners along the South Florida waterways. Promptly, three of the rebels were tied up by their hands, with feet dangling. They soon pled for mercy "& begged & stormed & cursed" but no one had any sympathy for them. An officer interferred, or they would have hung them then and there. At sunrise the next day, as flags flew at half staff and guns fired every half hour, Kitt recorded his feelings:

> Surely this is sorrow & joy mingled in the same cup for we also hear that the Rebels are laying down their arms everywhere and that some of the states are already preparing to come back into the Union. It looks as though peace [is] near us. We hope so and what a happy people we should be if only we had our beloved President to help inaugurate its reign.[56]

Only minimally and indirectly involved in war events at the time of Lincoln's death, many citizens of the dying Confederacy's southernmost state reacted in a similar way as the Federals—happiness that the war was ending and regret that Lincoln was dead and could not lead the country into peaceful years.

---

[56]Letter, Peter Kitts to Mrs. Case, 25 April 1865, Samuel Case Papers, Manuscript Department, William K. Perkins Library, Duke University.

In 1865 numerous farmers in Texas could be classified as "po' white." In their eyes Lincoln was the African American's champion and their hatred of him was boundless. Throughout the war years, Texas had been far removed from the centers of action in Virginia and along the Mississippi River. Only along the Gulf Coast where Texas was exposed to attacks of the U. S. Navy was the state in much peril. A small Union force occupied Galveston for a few months in 1862, and the port and terminus at Galveston only briefly. Texas remained relatively free of Union troops, and the state liberally contributed both men and provisions to the Southern cause. There was no formal surrender of the State of Texas—the Confederate Army and State Government simply melted away.[57]

Unbridled, vehemently pro-Confederate, and anti-Lincoln, Texas newspaper editors freely spoke their minds on all subjects as the war waged throughout the Confederate states. As the war progressed, it is impossible to exaggerate the role of the "fire-eating Texas editors" in fanning the flames of hatred of Lincoln and the horror Southerners felt they were suffering with Lincoln as President of the Union. During Lincoln's Presidency, Texas newspapers, uninhibited by Federal military control and bluntly partisan toward the "South's idyllic society," continued unabated their biased, virulent anti-Lincoln stories. When the one-sided, inflammatory accounts of Lincoln and developments in the sectional dispute reached Texas readers, all objectivity toward Lincoln quickly evaporated. When a Virginia newspaper editor commented that "Newspapers and Telegraphs have ruined the country. Suppress both and the country could be saved now," it could have well been applied to Texas newspapers. More than those of any other Southern state, Texas rebel papers expressed wild hatred of Lincoln and delirious glee at his murder. Texas newspapers accepted Lincoln's death as a major blessing.[58] The Texas *Republic* proclaimed, "It is certainly a

---

[57]T. R. Fehrenbach, *Lone Star: A History of Texas and the Texans* (New York: MacMillan, 1968), 351-352; Reynolds, *Editors Make War*, 98, 116.

[58]Ibid, 214-17; *Fredericksburg (Texas) Herald,* January 3, 1860; Ralph W. Steen, "Texas Newspapers and Lincoln," *Southwestern Historical Quarterly* 51 (January 1948) 3:199-212.

matter of congratulation that Lincoln is dead, because the world is happily rid of a monster that disgraced the form of humanity." The *Houston Telegraph* agreed when its editor wrote:

> From now until God's judgment day the minds of men will not cease to thrill at the killing of Abraham Lincoln. . . . It goes upon that high judgment roll for nations and for universal man with the slaying of Tarquin, of Caesar, of Charles I, Louis XVI, of Marot. . . . If the reign of despotism is again to be reinaugurated at this day and over this people, then let despotism and whoever may be its minion beware the deserved fate of the tyrants.[59]

One of the most respected papers in Texas, the *Galveston News* printed one of the most acrimonious editorials on Lincoln:

> Our country was bleeding and suffering from the war that [Lincoln's] party waged against it, and with deliberate malice he gloated over our sufferings and visited them on our own heads. We were the 'wicked man' and he, forsooth, was the instrument designed by providence for our punishment. On the 14th of April Abraham Lincoln was weltering in his own life blood, and the words *sic semper tyrannis* were ringing his death knell. In the plenitude of his power and arrogance he was struck down, and his soul ushered into eternity, with innumerable crimes to answer for. . . . It does look to us . . . as if an avenging Nemesis had brought swift and inevitable retribution upon a man stained with so many bloody crimes.[60]

When news of the assassination reached Dr. J. H. P. Baker, a Confederate Army doctor engaged in winding up his military hospital in Texas, he discussed it with his excited cohorts. In spite of what they

---

[59]*Houston Telegraph*, 26 April 1865.
[60]*Galveston News*, 28 April 1865.

had just read in the papers, all of which cursed Lincoln in harsh language, Baker and his friends had divided opinions. Baker felt that the South had had dark hours, but this was the darkest, and what the end would be, he could not fathom. He emphatically disapproved of such deeds as the assassination. It saddened him to come to the conclusion that it plainly manifested a "degenerate people" who are "fast drifting back to the age of the Caesars. . . . the hour darkens; is there to be no reaction?" he asked.[61]

Kate Stone, living in Texas at the time Lincoln died, continued to write in her journal:

> All honor to J. Wilkes Booth, who has rid the world of a tyrant and made himself famous for generations. It is a terrible tragedy, but what is war but one long tragedy? What torrents of blood Lincoln has caused to flow, and how Seward has aided him in his bloody work. I cannot be sorry for their fate. They deserve it. They have reaped their just reward.

Stone made no mention of tolling bells, public mourning, or black crepe, nor of what she thought of the traumatic, intense accounts of the assassination in Texas newspapers. Relatively free of direct military control of their daily lives, Texans did not assume the trappings and attitudes of "unfeigned regret" imposed on other Southerners by the armies of occupation, and relatively few Texans living on the cotton farms and prairies felt the need to turn to diaries and journals for personal expression of their inmost feelings.[62]

---

[61]Pocket Diary, entries dated 25-29 April 1965, Dr. F. H. P. Baker Papers, Joint Collection, University of Missouri Western Historical Manuscript Collection, Columbia, and State Historical Society of Missouri Manuscrips.

[62]Kate Stone [Sarah Katherine Stone Holmes], *Brokenburn: The Journal of Kate Stone, 1861-1868*, ed. John Q. Anderson (Baton Rouge: Louisiana State University Press, 1955), 332-333.

The Nation Mourns (The Lincoln Museum, Fort Wayne, Indiana, No. 4484)

Chapter 4

Reaction in
the Border States

In the months before the war, as Southern states were drawing
toward secession and the formation of the Confederacy, the
question of which side the border states—Maryland, Delaware,
Missouri, and Kentucky—would choose became a matter of deep
concern to both North and South. The border states were slaveholding,
but all had strong ties with the North. Antagonisms between the cotton
economy and the manufacturing interests existed in the borderland.
There were raging disputes and political differences between the pro-
Confederate and the pro-Union factions in all four border states.
Serious animosities existed between neighbors, between former friends
and associates, and most poignantly and permanently between family
members, who remained bitterly divided for generations, causing the
Civil War to be called the "Brothers' War." Such bitterness was
especially evident in the reactions of the people to Lincoln.[1]

After Lincoln's election and the fall of Sumter, Kentucky attempted
to remain neutral, but was grievously divided, with 30,000 Kentuckians
fighting for the South and some 64,000 for the Union cause. Three
times, but with little success, Kentucky was invaded by Confederate
armies seeking to rally the countryside to their cause. Lincoln considered his native Kentucky to be one of the pivotal states in the struggle.
He watched the state closely throughout the secession movement, and
he remarked that he hoped to have God on his side, but he *must* have
Kentucky. When Lincoln suggested compensated emancipation in July

---

[1]David M. Potter, *The South and the Sectional Conflict* (Baton Rouge: Louisiana
State University Press, 1968), 74-79.

1862, the Kentucky legislature acridly criticized the federal government for its long course of broken promises, with special venom toward President Lincoln, who with his government were "bent on the destruction of the Constitution and the Union." The storm of disapproval in Kentucky that broke over Lincoln and his administration had never been equalled up to that time. Few Kentuckians supported their native son. From the summer of 1864 Kentucky had been under martial law, and at the time of Lincoln's death, there was no sharp, clear sense that the fighting had ended. In retrospect, years later, some declared that "[T]he sympathy of the state was deeply touched [when Lincoln was shot], and a great transformation seems almost mysteriously to have swept over the people when word came that Lincoln was dead." If such a transformation did occur, it was not spontaneous.[2]

Similar to other areas of the South, immediately upon the announcement of Lincoln's assassination, Union officers issued orders in Kentucky for the proper observance of days of mourning, orders which were carried out by the military and the citizens in minute detail. Bells tolled throughout the state, businesses closed, public offices were draped in mourning crepe, public ceremonies and religious services memorializing the slain President were held. In public speeches, Unionist-Governor Thomas E. Bramlette paid high tribute to Lincoln, "as the savior of the nation . . . a man honest and utterly without guilt," and General J. M. Palmer called Lincoln "the purest man of the ages."[3] In Louisville, the editor of the *Democrat* thought the assassination must be a "cruel hoax . . . too horrible, surely, to be true." Another Louisvillian observed,

> The grief . . . at Lincoln's death was sincere, but the elaborately contrived funeral ceremonies were all part of a deliberate policy to keep the public stirred up over [the] assassination. The

---

[2]E. Merton Coulter, *The Civil War and Readjustment in Kentucky* (Chapel Hill: The University of North Carolina Press, 1926), 53, 158-159, 161.

[3]Ibid., 256-257; *Semi-Weekly Commonwealth*, 18 April 1865; *(Cincinnati) Gazette*, 18 April 1865.

Radicals who hoped to see stern punishment inflicted on the South were determined that Lincoln's lenient ideas should be burried with his lifeless body.[4]

While this might have been the case, the fact remains that as the word of Lincoln's death came to Kentucky, the hearts of many were genuinely touched, and their former attitudes toward Lincoln were changing; a gradual "transformation" did indeed occur.

Charles S. Todd, a distant relative of Mary Todd Lincoln, had just returned to his home in Owensboro when he received a letter from his friend, Lyman C. Draper. In his reply of 8 May 1865, Todd wrote,

> I mingle cordially in all your feelings growing out of the great national calamity. I was personally and politically devoted to Mr. Lincoln and I grieve for the irreparable loss his estimable widow has sustained, the more so as she is a distant relative, treating me with affection.[5]

John C. Underwood was another Kentuckian who had a personal interest in Lincoln. Although his father was a Unionist who had served as U. S. Senator from Kentucky, John "broke the traces" and went South, becoming an officer in the Confederate Army. He was taken prisoner by the Federals, but by special order of President Lincoln, presumably because of Lincoln's friendship with young Underwood's father, John was paroled. John proudly believed he was the "only personal prisoner the President had." When Lincoln died, Underwood declared with great feeling that the South "lost its best friend, and the

---

[4]Robert Emmett McDowell, *City of Conflict: Louisville in the Civil War, 1861-1865* (Louisville, Kentucky: Louisville Civil War Round Table, 1962), 199.

[5]Letter, C. S. Todd to Layman C. Draper, 8 May 1865, Draper Manuscripts, Charles S. Todd Papers, 1835-1876, State Historical Society of Wisconsin.

entire country one of its purest, broadest, and most noble presidents; and my parole will be returnable in Heaven."[6]

Many of Kentucky's newspaper editors—all operating under federal control when Lincoln died—reacted to the President's murder with great regret. The editor of the *Frankfort Commonwealth* penned a sad tribute to "our noble and beloved President," saying,

> In his heart there was no hate of the rebellious South—no feeling of revenge . . . no bitterness of spirit. . . . By hands of love he would draw back those of rebellion to their old alliance. . . . He has laid down his life for ours—he has fallen a martyr.[7]

Missouri, Delaware and Maryland were all torn by conflicting interests and the intense internal struggles. In Missouri, most of the African Americans were free, rather than slaves. In all three states the ratio of blacks-to-whites was relatively small compared to that in the eleven states of the Confederacy. During the war, most Missourians remained loyal to the federal government and to President Lincoln, whom Robert Yancey of Springfield called "the true and tried patriot and statesman. . . ."[8] Missouri voted against secession, but the state maintained a pro-Southern bias, and guerilla activities persisted throughout the war. It was not until after the war that Southern proclivities began to decline.

The morning of 15 April 1865 dawned gloriously over the rich lands of upper Missouri and the town of Warrensburg, where A. W. Reese, M.D. directed the operation of the United States hospital. The town had just received the happy news of Lee's surrender and plans

---

[6]Underwood Reminiscences, Manuscript Division, Kentucky Library, West Kentucky University, Bowling Green, 1-4; Michael Davis, *The Image of Lincoln in the South* (Knoxville: University of Tennessee Press, 1971), 105-134, passim.

[7]*Frankfort (Kentucky) Commonwealth*, 17-20 April 1865.

[8]Steve Yancey to Robert Yancey, 20 April 1865, Charles S. Yancey Letters, Joint Collection, University of Missouri Western Historical Manuscript Collection and State Historical Society of Missouri Collection.

were in progress to carry out orders received from Union Headquarters in St. Louis to celebrate the event. Reese took his little daughter by the hand and proceeded to the hillside where spectators assembled to watch the parade and military demonstrations. All faces (except those of the "sesesh") were lighted with joy when the gunners in their splendid blue and gold uniforms opened up volley after volley of cannon thunder. That night Reese gave orders to have the windows of the hospital illuminated. Early next morning, the hospital clerk, white-faced and agitated, rushed into Reese's office and threw the morning's dispatch upon his desk. "Mr. Lincoln. . . murdered last night!" he exclaimed. Profoundly affected, Reese later wrote his mother in words, nearly all of which were underlined: "Alas how soon was this great Nation plunged, from the Pinacle of rejoicing into the gloomy abyss of a sorrow that had no parallel in the annals of human history! How soon her happy bon-fires were quenched, and her shores enshrouded in the gloom of a universal sorrow! . . . Shall we not say that the name of John Wilkes Booth shall forever stand on the pages of American History as the perpetrator of the world's greatest crime?"

Preparations for further celebration of Grant's victory were suspended; businesses were closed; and the day of rejoicing was changed into one of mourning. In the town of Warrensburg the freedpersons were grief-stricken; with lamentations they mourned their greatest benefactor and friend. They invited Reese, together with General John McNeil to address them at a meeting called to express their grief at Lincoln's death. Standing under the shadow of the national flag "draped in the dark, funereal weeds of woe," and confronting the portrait of the martyred President, Reese spoke for more than an hour to "these poor creatures, just liberated from the shackles of bondage, and bowed with grief for their illustrious friend." At the conclusion of the speech, the freedmen sang, "Rally 'round the flag, boys," and the battle hymn, "John Brown's body lies mouldering in the grave."[9]

Not only in Warrensburg but also throughout the state of Missouri joyful celebrations of Grant's final victory in Virginia were interrupted by news of Lincoln's death. Sorrow and tears trod on the heels of joy. Silence and a special pall of gloom rested upon St. Louis. Men drifted together on the streets there, conversing in low and earnest tones. On Fourth Street a lone man murmured something as he passed by one crowd. Thinking that the man expressed pleasure at Lincoln's murder, the crowd turned upon him, seized him, beat him, and dragged him along the street. All the while the man screamed pleas to be heard. Finally, convinced that they had misunderstood what they thought had been his hearty approval of the murder, his attackers let him go.[10]

In other parts of Missouri in the days following Lincoln's death, others—pro-Lincoln and anti-Lincoln, pro-Union and anti-Union—expressed their diverse reactions to the murder. During those days, Jonathan B. Fuller, an itinerant Baptist preacher, continued to travel on the river boat and throughout the countryside of Missouri "preaching the gospel" as he had done throughout the war years. His sermons in the days after Lincoln's death were on the theme of the martyred President. He traveled on the steamer *Warsaw* for his preaching engagement at Hannibal. There he heard the "terrible news" of Lincoln's assassination, and when the congregation assembled to hear him preach, all the faces of the large crowd of people in attendance were covered with gloom. At LaGrange, bells tolled incessantly, business ceased, houses and flags were draped in black. At the Methodist Episcopal Church in LaGrange, Fuller was joined by two other Protestant ministers, all three of whom gave stirring addresses to the full house on the subject of the dead leader. Fuller's address was well received. He took as his text Revelation 21:1: "[A]nd I saw a new

---

[9]A. W. Reese, Personal Recollections, typed copy. Joint Collection University of Missouri Western Historical Manuscript Collection, Columbia, and State Historical Society of Missouri Collection, 219-228, including letters dated 16 and 26 April 1865.

[10]Galusha Anderson, *The Story of a Border City During the Civil War: A Political History* (Wilmington, Delaware: Historical Society of Delaware, 1961), 361-363.

heaven and a new earth: for the first heaven and the first earth were passed away; and there was no more sea." Later Fuller penned the following words in precise penmanship in his meticulously kept journal:

> House full. I delivered the Address which was well received. Four years ago not six of the throng would have gone ten steps to do the murdered statesman honor. Tempore muta[n]tur (Times are changing.).[11]

In Delaware, unlike Missouri, the number of slaves in the state had declined in the early nineteenth century, while the number of free blacks had increased. In the course of Lincoln's presidency, pro-Southern feeling increased rather than diminished in Delaware. Few saw eye-to-eye with Lincoln's decisions, and the state did not support the Emancipation Proclamation.[12]

At least one Delaware lady received the news with gladness. When Lee surrendered, the *Georgetown Union* welcomed the news with large headlines: "Glory, Glory, Hallelujah—Retribution. Our Colored Troops the First to Enter the Doomed City." Anna Ferris expressed her "glowing gratitude" for victory. In Smyrna, the lights from the brilliant illumination "glowed on faces that looked happy," and "people generally went crazy over the glorious news."[13]

At Fort Delaware where a large number of rebel prisoners were being held in April 1865, Union prison guards and officers-in-charge of the prisoners followed orders from headquarters in expressing profound mourning for the slain President. The prisoners themselves,

---

[11]Jonathan B. Fuller Papers, Joint Collection, University of Missouri Western Historical Manuscript Collection, Columbia, and State Historical Society of Missouri Collection, Journal entries, 14-19 April 1865.

[12]Harold Bell Hancock, *Delaware During the Civil War: A Political History* (Wilmington, Delaware: Historical Society of Delaware, 1961), 85, 91, 133, 137.

[13]Ibid., 157, 159; Anna Ferris Diary, entry of 19 April 1865, Ferris Papers, Friends' Historical Society, Swarthmore, Pennsylvania; *Georgetown (Delaware) Union*, 7 April 1865; Delaware *Gazette*, 11 April 1865.

as expressed by one of them, "with the noble generosity native to Southern character, [hid] all resentment" at Lincoln's death. There were many expressions of condemnation of the "horrible murder of our beloved President," and of the "foulest deed that ever [sullied] the name of humanity." There were few open expressions of approval of the removal of the President. Although there was strong Confederate sympathy in two of the three counties of Delaware, the state did stay in the Union, and Confederate sympathizers were relatively much more circumspect.[14]

In Maryland, dissonant voices tell of a state torn between North and South, between Lincoln, the Union, and emancipation and secession, slavery, and states' rights. As the nation edged toward war, Maryland was severely divided. Some rejected just about everything that Lincoln and his cohorts did to keep Maryland in the Union, including the occupations of Baltimore and Annapolis by Union troops early in the war. Nevertheless, Marylanders fought on both sides. As in other border states, families were often split.

Baltimore had been the scene of an early assassination plot against President-elect Lincoln as he traveled to Washington some days before his first inauguration. Concerned with a plot's possible success Lincoln's advisors convinced him, in a decision he later regretted, secretly to board a different train in Baltimore and enter the capital undetected. Now at war's end the city was caught up in the wave of exultation that swept through the North in early April 1865. When Lee surrendered joy was tumultuous in Baltimore, though not universal. The loud and constant pealing of church and town bells sometimes sounded above the cheers of assembled merrymakers in the center of the city, while detachments of Federal infantry watched benignly. Noises from small street fights sometimes pierced the merrymaking, fights that engaged

---

[14]Robert E. Park, "Diary of Robert E. Park, Twelfth Alabama Regiment," *Southern Historical Papers* 3 (June 1877) 6:245-54, see entry of 3 June 1877.

the attention of the Federals. Upon their firm suggestion, some Secessionists "acted happy," waving small Stars and Stripes.[15]

On Saturday morning, April 15, the bells of Baltimore abruptly changed their tune. Lincoln was dead. Doleful, prolonged knells overrode the sounds of driving rain. The next day in their pulpits clergymen replaced their usual Easter sermons with eulogies of Lincoln, and after services and throughout the afternoon, the streets became deserted and still. When one Maryland citizen broke the calm of the day openly to endorse Booth's act, he suffered the ignominy of having his head shaved and was whipped with rawhide straps. Baltimore was Booth's home town, and while the city's streets had been crowded with mourners, an enterprising photographer "conspicuous for his disloyalty" posted the assassin's likeness and "other obnoxious pictures" in front of his establishment. When the crowds heard of them, their anger flared and they quickly converged on the place. The proprietor hurriedly gathered up his goods and retreated behind a line of the Provost Marshal's men, who were "hard put" to preserve the peace.[16]

There were many Marylanders in Union forces stationed throughout the Southern states when, first, the news of Lee's surrender, then of Lincoln's death permeated their ranks. Union soldiers committed their thoughts to paper, in letters home or in their diaries. Charles Griswold, a native Marylander, and his buddies received the news of Lee's surrender with almost boundless joy, and the news of the "loss of our beloved President" with almost boundless grief. The Unionists in the South who were in uniform did not express their emotions over the momentous events as publicly as did those in the northern states, but they felt both keenly, Griswold believed. "No one loved Abraham Lincoln better than his soldiers and none felt more deeply his loss," Griswold wrote in a letter to his sister back home in Maryland. He concluded his letter with the words:

---

[15]Carl Bode, *Maryland: A Bicentennial History* (New York: W. W. Norton, 1977), 123, 132, 133. The quotation "brightest epoch. . . " is from Thomas Scharf, *Chronicle of Baltimore*, 633, as quoted by Bode, 133.

[16]Wiley, "Billy Yank and Abraham Lincoln," 119; *(Kansas City) Daily Journal*, 18 April 1865.

Even his enemies respected him and mourned his death. I mean those who have taken up arms against him and his Country. I know he had enemies at the North but they were not worth the name of enemies . . . We should be thankful that we found such a man and that he was spared to us so long.[17]

William Wilkens Glenn was born in Baltimore. Literate and loquacious, he was described by John C. Calhoun as one of the most respectable and intelligent citizens of the city. He "traveled on the fringes of grand events, on familiar terms with the great and near great" throughout the states and in Europe as well. Harboring strong pro-Southern and anti-Lincoln-administration views, he purchased controlling interest in the Baltimore *Daily Exchange* as a medium for influencing public opinion in Maryland and rallying supporters to the Southern cause. His editorial policy resulted in his arrest in September 1861 and his newspaper was suppressed. Upon his release from Fort McHenry a few months later, he turned his energies toward an active underground campaign to aid the Southern cause. His subversive activities centered largely on smuggling persons into the South. Unable to express his opinions and policies in his suppressed newspaper, he took to writing prolific accounts of events and his personal views and interpretation of them in journals that have only in recent years been brought together and published.[18]

Glenn's personal reactions to Lincoln's assassination likely reflected the sentiments of many other Marylanders and pro-Southern citizens of the border areas. On April 16, 1865, Glenn wrote in his journal:

News came late last night . . . of the assassination of Lincoln and Seward . . . The excitement [in New York City] soon

---

[17]Letter, Charles Griswold to Sister Lucy, 4 May 1865, Edward Griswold and Joel Griswold Papers, 1862-1865, Manuscript Department, William R. Perkins Library, Duke University.

[18]William Wilkins Glenn, *Between North and South: A Maryland Journalist Views the Civil War*, ed. Bayley Ellen Marks and Mark Norton Schatz (Teaneck, NJ: Fairleigh Dickinson University Press, 1976), 9-11.

became great. In Wall St. it was intense; so much so that business was stopped & many houses entirely closed. . . . One boy who declared it served Lincoln right was beaten. . . . Later another man was mobbed for thinking Lincoln's death a good thing. . . . At the corner of Wall & William St. orations were delivered from the high steps. Butler speaking and advocation [sic] death, destruction & fire & sword for the South. . . . By noon all of Broadway was draped in mourning. The streets were filled. . . . [B]lood and thunder men swore that Grant should be censured for paroling one single rebel in Virginia. [They said that] he should feed them on saw dust till the heart was starved out of them. . . .

At present there is but one feeling on the subject—and no one dares speak otherwise. After some thought I have come to a different conclusion. Seward is the man who for years has nursed and fostered and fed this irrepressible conflict, till it has grown to be the monster which is preying upon the country. Lincoln is the man who had aided and abetted & encouraged the schemes of Seward, and by his unscrupulous cunning and shrewd duplicity has succeeded in dragging down the Nation far lower than Seward ever anticipated. Lincoln was elected President under the constitution. After four years of war during which crimes have been committed, by his permission & with his approval, which would have disgraced Nero, he steps into his [job] as dictator. This is the plain fact. The people of the North are only fit for a Despotical form of government. They feel it; but so great has been the influence of republican education on the minds of men that no man has been found sufficiently bold to throw off the ideas which control him[,] grasp the sceptre and destroy free institutions. But the position which no bold man would strike for Lincoln has sneaked into—and there he was barricading & fortifying himself every day. I much doubt if Andy Johnson can start where Lincoln left off. . . .

As far as the South is concerned, I cannot see that she is going to be really the loser, although extreme measures will prevail and much suffering will occur. . . . The South is to be kept in subjugation by armed negroes. They are to have equal rights with the Whites and the muskets of the armed force and the votes of their brethren are to crush the power of southern aristocracy. What could be worse than that?

The history of this war has yet to be written. It is a great social revolution. This assassination is another great step.[19]

Glenn was back in Baltimore when he wrote on April 21 that Lincoln's corpse passed through the city that day. The procession passed up Eutaw Street, which was densely lined with spectators. Black Masons joined in the procession. All the blacks in town were agitated; house servants refused to work. As for Glenn himself, at ten in the morning of 21 April, he draped one window with crepe—at three in the afternoon he promptly removed it, thus following orders for mourning as prescribed by the military. Glenn's family thought he was wrong in not leaving the crepe up longer. Late that afternoon, his house was almost the only one in Baltimore without some symbol of mourning.[20]

---

[19]Ibid., 196-197, journal entries of 16 and 21 April 1865.
[20]Ibid., 203.

All over the country, mourning badges like this worn by millions of persons, including school children in the funeral procession. (The Lincoln Museum, Fort Wayne, Indiana, No. 2709)

Conclusion

A biding love of the South united rebels in an unshakable bond. Many Southerners despised Lincoln and detested everything for which he stood. But their hatred of Lincoln never eclipsed their regard for their beloved South. In great stress, they fought as one to sustain the South; they fought to alleviate whatever to their individual ways of thinking threatened their South. Almost all were animated by a conviction of the rightness of the Southern cause as they saw it. Almost all resented Lincoln, the leader of "Yankee meddling" in Southern affairs. Few experienced genuine grief at Lincoln's assassination; yet many felt that the South would fare worse under Andrew Johnson as President than under Lincoln if he had lived.

Southerners reacted to Lincoln's assassination in terms of Lincoln the President—a threat to the South, to their property, to their lives. Their various feelings toward the living President and their reaction to his death differed in significant ways. Reactions differed by region, by locale of the writer. In the deep South, where love of the South was most tenacious and where slave ownership and the proportion of blacks-to-whites was largest, Lincoln appeared as a great threat. He was viewed by those in the deep South as a menace to the Southern "way of life," to their own lives and to their property—especially to their slave property. Many in the deep South were smugly pleased, if not joyful, when they received the news of Lincoln's assassination. Although gladdened at the news, they attempted to dissociate themselves from the assassin—a Southerner—and they disclaimed responsibility for the crime. Out of fear of retaliation, they openly expressed little joy when Lincoln died. They went along with token expressions of grief and observed the enemy's orders for ceremonial display of mourning. They feared that Andrew Johnson would be an even worse President, more malicious and vindictive than Lincoln would have been had he lived. Of the citizens of the Deep South states—Alabama, Georgia, Mississippi, South Carolina, Louisiana, Florida, Texas—only Texas and Florida citizens reacted somewhat differently from the others. Since there were few if any Union forces in

Texas at the time of Lincoln's death, many Texans openly expressed a maniacal glee without fear of recrimination; Floridians were only minimally and indirectly involved in war events at the time of Lincoln's death. They reacted to the assassination news with neither fanfare and joy, nor with mourning and sorrow. Few Floridians had strong feelings about Lincoln's death or took up their pens to note their feelings. For the most part, whatever their feelings, they expressed their reactions openly to their friends and cohorts and in newspapers that had not come under Union control.

In the upper South where slavery was not central to the subregion's economy, and where the ratio of blacks-to-whites smaller than in the Deep South, many reacted with shock and regret to the news of Lincoln's death. As in the Deep South, there was concern that Lincoln's "tyrannical deeds" would be followed by even worse under Andrew Johnson. In that regard, upper South Confederates believed that Lincoln's death was far from being desirable for them. They were not joyful at Lincoln's death. Some were even horrified, but somehow they could not sincerely grieve. They felt that the whole South would be held responsible for the outrage that they not only disowned but deplored. Although few expressed any great fear of the new President, they considered Johnson "a more vindictive man" than Lincoln.

Citizens of the border states—Maryland, Delaware, Missouri and Kentucky—were widely divergent in their attitudes toward Lincoln's assassination. Those who were loyal to the Union and to Lincoln were most often "pitched into the gloomy abyss of sorrow" at the news of Lincoln's demise, and they doubted Johnson's ability to carry on the government where Lincoln left off at his death. Those with Southern proclivities most often reacted with satisfaction, or joy, but with fear of what would happen next. They tended to keep their thoughts to themselves, even among family members and associates, for families were often bitterly divided in their loyalties to the Union or the Confederacy, and in their reaction to Lincoln's demise. But Northern and Southern sympathizers in the border states shared a feeling of uneasiness of what the future held for the reunited nation without Lincoln at the helm.

Beside differences in attitude toward Lincoln's assassination between regions of the South, other patterns of attitudes toward Lincoln's death emerge from the study. There were differences of reaction according to occupation or standing of the people of the South. The wealthy slaveholding planter was most often glad of Lincoln's death. Through the Emancipation Proclamation Lincoln had divested the slaveowner of his most valuable property, namely, his slaves. Because of this, in the eyes of many slaveowners, Lincoln "got what he deserved." On the other hand, the farmer who owned few if any slaves, as well as the poverty-stricken mountaineer and back countryman in remote areas of the South reacted with relative indifference. They expressed the opinion that it was just as well that "Old Abe" was gone: now he couldn't "meddle" with the South's business anymore, and the "govmint" would continue to function.

Editors of Southern papers under the control of the Unionists at the time of Lincoln's death almost unanimously expressed profound regret in the columns of their papers. Editors of the few anti-Lincoln newspapers that were still free of enemy control—mainly those in Texas—printed columns expressing glee and the thought that Lincoln's demise was a "major blessing." Most clergymen under the constraints of enemy orders preached eulogizing sermons, declaring the murder "a dishonor to Almighty God." Others, a Catholic priest among them, rationalized that the murder of Lincoln "for religious purposes" was justified.

The opinions of women left at home while their men fought on the battlefield differed from the reactions of men who served the Confederacy in uniform. Women were especially diligent in keeping diaries and writing letters in which they expressed abhorrence of the crime, but they were glad "Ole Abe" was gone, for he had caused "torrents of blood to flow." They were sure the murder was justified. The assassin deserved "all honor." They prayed for mercy "on those who did it." They bitterly regretted the necessity to pretend grief for the slain President, grief they did not feel.

The first reaction of men who were still prisoners-of-war in Union camps, or who had been paroled at the time they heard the news of Lincoln's death, differed from that of their womenfolk. Feelings of satisfaction swept over the prisoners when they heard the "good news," feelings that were quickly supplanted by fear for their lives. After the prisoners were released and the threat of retaliation by their captors had passed, many came to believe that their fate would have been easier if Lincoln had been spared to guide the affairs of the nation than it would be under Johnson. They came to regret Lincoln's death. Confederate soldiers who had not been prisoners and who were returning home at the time of the assassination reacted almost immediately to the news with the thought that the war would now be pursued more barbarously than ever, for they distrusted Andrew Johnson, a despicable "Tennessean turncoat" in their eyes.

One Southern lawyer felt that the assassination would result in benefit to the South and secure for the South a separate nationality; other lawyers rejoiced that Lincoln could no longer raise his howl of diabolical triumph over the South. Still others expressed various degrees of grief or joy. Few lawyers were indifferent.

From the eldest white-haired ex-slave to the youngest black children, all felt that they had lost their best friend on earth. Marse Lincoln was their savior; he had saved them from bondage. Now he was gone. What would become of them? The blacks whose freedom was at the center of the controversy reacted with sobs and loud lamentation. They feared they would become slaves again. Not all free blacks and black leaders shared the former slaves' grief. Some were disgusted by what they considered to be Lincoln's uncertain attitude toward slavery. Some, now that Lincoln was dead, began to hatch plans for a "Negro State."

In 1960 Richard Current made a wise and succinct observation in an address on the current state of Lincoln scholarship. "There are . . . some controversies about Lincoln that may never be put to rest," he said. "Some controversies are rooted largely in emotion, not entirely in reason, and hence not quite amenable to objective fact or impartial thought." He further noted that

> Lincoln scholarship will be advanced mainly by the further
> exploitation of manuscript collections and other sources whose

existence already is known. What is needed in some cases is no more than a careful study of materials which in the past have been rather heedlessly used. What is needed in other cases . . . [is] a historian's imagination that can see new patterns of meanings in evidence already familiar."[1]

Southerners' reactions to Lincoln's assassination as expressed in their personal papers are already familiar. Indeed, they are largely rooted in emotion; certainly not entirely in reason. There is one clear, general pattern of meaning that emerges from the study of manuscripts and newspapers available in Southern repositories. Whatever the individual feelings of Southerners were toward Lincoln and whatever their individual reactions to his murder—whether they rejoiced or grieved, feared or welcomed the leadership of Johnson, their love of the South overrode all other emotions.

In an article, "A Southerner Views Lincoln," published in February 1928 in *Scribner's Magazine*, Archibald Rutledge gave his impression of how Lincoln was regarded below the Mason-Dixon line at that time. Lincoln, he said, was viewed "with a good deal of kindness." He predicted that more and more Southerners would see Lincoln in these terms: "For it is a glory of our common humanity that we cannot escape loving one who is great of heart."[2] Rutledge's prophesy has come to pass.

---

[1] Richard Nelson Current, *Speaking of Abraham Lincoln: The Man and His Meaning for Our Times* (Urbana and Chicago: University of Illinois Press, 1983), 46, 47. The quotation is from "The Lincoln Theme—Unexhausted and Inexhaustible," an address at a symposium on "The Current State of Lincoln Scholarship," Library of Congress, Washington, D.C., 11 February 1960.

[2] Archibald Rutledge, "A Southerner Views Lincoln," *Scribner's Magazine* 83 (February 1928).

A Note on Sources

To my knowledge no book-length account of Southern reaction to Lincoln's assassination has been published, nor have the manuscript collections and periodical materials I perused been previously researched for the purpose. Michael Davis's *The Image of Lincoln in the South* (Knoxville: University of Tennessee Press, 1971) addresses the subject but does not exhaust it. In his book, Davis explores and documents changing Southern attitudes toward Lincoln, and he examines elements of the Lincoln legend to which Southerners responded favorably. He speculates on the reasons for changing attitudes toward Lincoln after his death, and he presents commonly held views of Lincoln that he saw reflected in newspaper reports and selected writings by Southerners. The chapter, "The Confederates' Lincoln" inspired me to delve more deeply into the unpublished materials in diaries and journals that became available to me, and to mine more thoroughly the writings of Southerners through which I could trace attitudes expressed at the time of his assassination. I found Davis's book a challenging point of departure for my work.

Thomas Reed Turner's volume, *Beware the People Weeping: Public Opinion and the Assassination of President Lincoln* (Baton Rouge: Louisiana State University Press, 1982) reexamines Lincoln's assassination and the conspiracies in the context of their historical setting. In the chapter entitled, "Southern Reaction to Lincoln's Assassination," Turner observes that "historians have felt little need to investigate how and why people reacted as they did." He deplores the fact that although the historiography of the assassination is voluminous, historians have given too little attention to the historical setting, to understanding events adequately as they occurred. With Turner's thoughtful observations in mind, I became more sensitive to details of the historical milieu of the Confederate South, and to those specific decisions and events in Lincoln's life that influenced Southern reaction to his murder.

My study of Southern reaction to Lincoln's assassination is based on and structured around family papers contained in manuscript collections in several universities and colleges, in national and state archives, and in special collections of public and private libraries. The principal sources were diaries, letters, memoirs, farm journals, memoranda and sermons, as well as Southern newspapers and periodicals extant during the Civil War period. The materials were mined from the Southern Historical Collection, Wilson Library, University of North Carolina, Chapel Hill; Department of Archives and Manuscripts and the Lincoln Collection, Louisiana State University Libraries; the Woodson Research Center of the Fondren Library, Rice University, and the Clayton Genealogical Library, Houston; William R. Perkins Library, Manuscript Department, Emory University; Special Collections, Western Kentucky University; Manuscripts and Rare Book Department, The College of William and Mary; the Heritage Room Collections, Huntsville, Alabama Public Library; Manuscript Division and Historic Newpaper Files of the Library of Congress; the Georgia Department of Archives and History; and the Alabama Department of Archives and History. Specific, named manuscripts and materials from these and other collections which contributed to the study are listed in the Bibliography.

The manuscript collections, most of which I visited and researched personally, were my major source, supplemented by published memoirs and biographies. The collections listed in "Manuscripts" in the bibliography have at least one diary, letter, journal, paper, or pocket-sized daybook in which the writer expressed opinions of Lincoln and how he or she felt about the President's assassination. Sometimes the entries were composed of only a few sentences or words; in several instances I was able to trace an individual's attitudes toward Lincoln in diaries in which entries were made throughout the war years. Robert Manson Myers, ed., *The Children of Pride* (New Haven: Yale University Press, 1972) chronicles the lives of one Southern family through their letters, written before, during, and after the Civil War. It is a unique, superbly edited, and much prized source by which I could trace the reactions to Lincoln of many family members and could gain a better understanding of why they and other Southerners of the planter class reacted to the assassination as they did. Numerous other diaries, edited and published since the war, especially diaries and letters of Southern women, as well as of Confederate prisoners of war and Union soldiers stationed in occupied Southern towns, furnished me with essential material. Among the biographies and published memoirs that I found of particular value were *Mary Boykin Chesnut: A Diary from Dixie* (New York: Peter Smith Company, 1919) and *Mary Chesnut's Civil War*, ed. C. Vann Woodward (New Haven: Yale University Press, 1981); *The Private War of Lizzie Hardin*, ed. G. Glenn Clift (Frankfort: The Kentucky Historical Society, 1965); and W. H. Morgan, *Personal Reminiscences of the War of 1861-1865* Lynchburg, Virginia: J. P. Bell and Company, 1911).

Of the many general works on the life of Lincoln and his relationship with the South, I have included in the Bibliography only those from which I have drawn factual material, or that had some bearing on my interpretation. By far the most helpful were James G. Randall and Richard N. Current, *Lincoln, the President: Last Full Measure* (New York: Dodd, Mead, 1955); James G. Randall, *Lincoln and the South* (Baton Rouge: Louisiana State University Press, 1946); Stephen B. Oates, *With Malice Toward None: The Life of Abraham Lincoln* (New York: Harper and Row, 1977); Richard N. Current, *The Lincoln Nobody Knows* (New York: McGraw-Hill, 1958); Stephen B. Oates, *Abraham Lincoln: The Man Behind the Myth* (New York: Harper and Row, 1984), and David Herbert Donald, *Lincoln* (New York: Simon and Schuster, 1996).

I kept Mark E. Neely's *The Abraham Lincoln Encyclopedia* (New York: McGraw Hill, 1982) by my right hand throughout the two years I worked on the book. It was constantly provocative, and my major, indispensable reference for information about Lincoln.

In assessing the influence of Southern newspapers on the reaction of Southerners to the assassination, I received special benefit from J. Cutler Andrews, *The South Reports the Civil War* (Princeton, N.J.: Princeton University Press, 1970); Donald E. Reynolds, *Editors Make War: Southern Newspapers in the Secession Crisis* (Nashville: Vanderbilt University Press, 1970); Hodding Carter, *Their Words were Bullets: The Southern Press in War, Reconstruction, and Peace* (Athens: University of Georgia Press, 1969); Herbert Mitgang, *Abraham Lincoln: A Press*

Portrait (Chicago, Quadrangle Books, 1971). As the war progressed and many Southern newspapers came under the control of the Union, the "rebel" papers that did not suspend publication, radically changed editorial policies. In tracing the changing policies and attitudes toward Lincoln of specific Southern newspapers, I found value in J. Cutler Andrews, "The Confederate Press and Public Morale," *The Journal of Southern History* 32 (November 1966) 4; Richard Bardolf, "Malice Toward One—Lincoln and the North Carolina Press," *Lincoln Herald* 53 (Winter 1952) 4; Ralph W. Steen, "Texas Newspapers and Lincoln," *The Southern Historical Quarterly* 51 (January 1948) 3:199-212; John E. Talmadge, "Savannah's Yankee Newspapers," *Georgia Review* 12 (Spring 1958); Rabun L. Brantley, *Georgia Journalism in the Civil War Period* (Nashville, Tennessee: George Peabody College for Teachers, 1929); and in Thomas Ewing Dabney, *One Hundred Years: The Story of the Times Picayune from Founding to 1940* (Baton Rouge: Louisiana State University Press, 1944).

Of the journal articles that discuss reactions in an individual Southern state, or that consider various pertinent aspects of Lincoln's life that have a bearing on attitudes toward the assassination, I found the following most useful: Martin Abbott, "Southern Reaction to Lincoln's Assassination," *Abraham Lincoln Quarterly*, 7 (September 1952) 3:111-127; Avery Craven, "Southern Attitudes toward Abraham Lincoln," *Papers in Illinois History*, Transaction of the Illinois State Historical Society, 1942;Robert F. Durden, "A. Lincoln: Honkie or Equalitarian?" *South Atlantic Quarterly* 7 (Summer 1972) 281-291; J. G. deRoulhac Hamilton, "Lincoln and the South," *Sewannee Review* 17 (April 1909) 128-135; John W. Inzer, "How the News of the Assassination of President Lincoln was Received by Confederate Prisoners on Johnson's Island in April, 1865," *The Gulf States Historical Magazine*, 1 (July 1901 to May 1903): 194-198; R. L. Reid, "Louisiana and Lincoln's Assassination, Reactions in a Southern State," *The Southern Historian* 6 (Spring 1985): 20-27; Archibald Rutledge, "A Southerner Views Lincoln," *Scribner's* 83 (February 1928): 204-213.

Bibliography

Manuscript Collections

Alabama State Archives, Montgomery, Alabama, William Cooper Diaries.
Auburn University, Auburn, Alabama, Department of Archives James Mallory Journal (1843-1877).
Birmingham (Alabama) Public Library, Department of Archives, J. Morgan Smith Correspondence (1842-1901).
College of William and Mary, Williamsburg, Virginia, Manuscript Department
    Joseph E. Johnson Papers (1865).
    William Lamb Diary (1865).
    Powell Family Papers (1865).
Duke University, Durham, North Carolina, Perkins Library, Manuscript Department
    Charles S. Brown Papers.
    Samuel Case Papers.
    Washington Sandford Chaffin Papers, "Brief Journal," April and May, 1865.
    Clanton Papers, Diary of Ella Gertrude (Clanton) Thomas, typed copy, pp. 66-69.
    Sarah Morgan Dawson Diary.
    George Washington Flowers Memorial Collection, Edgar Dinsmore Correspondence.
    Eltinge-Lord Family Papers, Correspondence, 1865.
    Fletcher Papers (1816-1968), Lucy Muse (Walton) Fletcher Diary, 1865.
    Edward Griswold and Joel Griswold Papers (1862-1865).
    William Arnold Spicer Papers, Diary, 1865.
    Joseph Julius Wescoat Diary (1863-1865).
    Aaron Wilbur Papers, 1865 Correspondence.
Emory University, Atlanta, Georgia, Robert W. Woodruff Library, Special Collections.

Gourdin Young Papers.
Hartstuff Journal.
Friends Historical Society, Swathmore, Pennsylvania
Ferris Papers, Anna Ferris Diary, 1865.
Georgia State Archives, Atlanta, Georgia
Bryan/Willingham/Lawton Papers, Letter dated May 24, 1865.
Lavender Ray Diary, 1865.
Huntsville (Alabama) Public Library, Heritage Room
Edna Keel, Master's Thesis, "History of the Newspapers of Huntsville, Alabama." Typed copy.
Lawson McGhee Library, Knoxville, Tennessee
McClung Collection, William Barton Reynolds Papers.
Library of Congress. Rare Books and Special Collections Division
Edmund Ruffin Diary.
Natchez *Courier* pamphlet dated April 19, 1865.
Louisiana State University, Baton Rouge, Department of Archives and Manuscripts
Louis A. Bringlier and Family Papers.
Isaac Erwin Diary, 1848-1868, typescript copy.
Mary Alice Hebert, "Louisiana Journalism of the Civil War Period," Masters Thesis, typescript, 1937.
Thomas Thomson Taylor Papers, 1861-1866.
State Historical Society of Wisconsin
Draper Manuscripts, Charles S. Todd Papers, 1835-1876.
W. C. Moffett Diary, 1865.
University of Georgia (Athens), Manuscript Collection
William Starr Basinger papers, "The Savannah Volunteer Guards."
University of Kentucky (Lexington) Library, Special Collection
Dobbins Papers.
University of Missouri (Columbia), Historical Manuscript Collection, Columbia, and State Historical Society of Missouri Manuscripts, Joint Collections.
Dr. J. H. P. Baker Papers.
Henry C. Fiske Diaries, Volume 3, 1865.
Jonathan B. Fuller Papers, Journal entries for 1865.

Dr. William Lomax Papers.

Dr. A. W. Reese, "Personal Recollections."

Charles S. Yancey Letters, 1865.

University of North Carolina, Southern Historical Collection

Chadick Diary, 1865.

Eltinge-Lord Family Papers.

John Johnson Papers, Diaries, 1865.

Edward McCrady L'Engle Papers, Correspondence, 1865.

Stephen Mallory Papers, Diary, 1865.

Schenck Papers, Typed copy of 1865 Journal.

William H. Stewart Diary.

Waddell Papers, Susannah Gordon Waddell Diary.

Haigh Papers, "Diary of a Rebel Prisoner", 1865.

LeConte Papers, Emma LeConte Diary, 1865.

Western Kentucky University (Bowling Green), Manuscript Division,

Kentucky Library

Underwood Reminiscences.

Newspapers

Atlanta (Georgia) Daily Intelligencer.

Augusta (Georgia) Chronicle and Sentinel.

Augusta (Georgia) Constitutionalist.

Charleston (South Carolina) South Carolina Courier.

Charleston (South Carolina) Mercury.

Cincinnati (Ohio) Gazette.

Fayetteville (North Carolina) Semi-Weekly Gazelle.

Frankfort (Kentucky) Commonwealth.

Galveston (Texas) News.

Georgetown (Delaware) Union.

Houston (Texas) Telegraph.

Kansas City (Missouri) Daily Journal.

Knoxville (Tennessee) Whig and Rebel Ventilator.

Little Rock (Arkansas) Gazette.

Louisville (Kentucky) Democrat.

Macon (Georgia) Daily Telegraph.
Memphis (Tennessee) Appeal.
Nashville (Tennessee) Union and American.
New Bern (North Carolina) Times.
New Orleans (Louisiana) Black Republican.
New Orleans (Louisiana) Daily Delta.
New Orleans (Louisiana) Daily Picayune.
New Orleans (Louisiana) Picayune.
New Orleans (Louisiana) Times.
New Orleans (Louisiana) Tribune.
New Orleans (Louisiana) Weekly Times.
New York Herald.
New York Times.
Petersburg (Florida) Daily Express.
Raleigh (North Carolina) Church Intelligencer.
Raleigh (North Carolina) Semi-Weekly Standard.
Raleigh (North Carolina) Standard
Raleigh (North Carolina) Weekly Journal.
Richmond (Virginia) Dispatch.
Richmond (Virginia) Enquirer.
Salisbury (North Carolina) Daily Union Banner.
San Antonio (Texas) Ledger and Texas.
Savannah (Georgia) Daily Herald.
Savannah (Georgia) Morning News.
Savannah (Georgia) Republican
Shreveport (Louisiana) Semi-Weekly.
Wilmington (North Carolina) Daily Journal.
Wilmington (North Carolina) Herald of the Union.

Articles

Abbott, Martin. "Southern Reaction to Lincoln's Assassination," *Abraham Lincoln Quarterly*, 7 (September 1952) 3:111-127.
Andrews, J. Cutler. "The Confederate Press and Public Morale," *Journal of Southern History*, 32 (November, 1966) 4:463.

Baker, Thomas H. "Refugee Newspaper: The Memphis *Daily Appeal*, 1862-1865," *Journal of Southern History*, 29 (August 1963): 326-343.

Bardolf, Richard. "Malice Toward One—Lincoln in the North Carolina Press," *Lincoln Herald*, 53 (Winter, 1952): 4:43.

Braden, Waldo W. "Kindly Let Me be Silent: A Reluctant Lincoln," *Lincoln Herald*, 86 (Winter, 1984): 195-201.

Cawthon, John A. "Letters of a North Carolina Private to his Wife, 1862-1865," *Mississippi Valley Historical Review*. 30 (1943-1944): 533-550.

Chadick, Mrs. W.D. "Civil War Days in Huntsville: A Diary by Mrs. W. D. Chadwick [sic]," *Alabama Historical Quarterly* 9 (1947): 2:324-333.

Coulter, E. Merton. "What the South Has Done about her History," *Journal of Southern History* 2 (February 1836): 3-28.

Craven, Avery. "Southern Attitudes Toward Abraham Lincoln," *Papers in Illinois History. Transactions of the Illinois State Historical Society*, 1942, 2-18.

Crenshaw, Edward, "Diary of Captain Edward Crenshaw of the Confederate State Army," *Alabama Historical Quarterly* 2 (Winter 1940): 4:465-471.

Durden, Robert F. "A. Lincoln: Honkie or Equalitarian?" *South Atlantic Quarterly* 7 (Summer 1972): 281-291.

Elder, Bishop William Henry. "The Bishop of Natchez on the Death of Lincoln," Willard E. Wight, ed. *Lincoln Herald* 58 (Fall 1956): 13-14.

"Expressions of the Freedmen, Office of Freedmen, Hilton Head Island, South Carolina, at a Meeting of the Council of Administration Held at Mitchellville Yesterday, 21 April 1865, Commemorative of the Assassination of Pres. Lincoln," *The Liberator* 35 (May 5, 1865) 18. Microfilm.

Gay, William H. "Reminiscences of Abraham Lincoln, Quincy, and the Civil War," *Journal of Illinois History* 7 (October) i: 248-261.

Gregorie, Ann King, ed. "Diary of Captain Joseph Julius Wescoat, 1863-1865," *South Carolina Historical Magazine* 59 (January-April 1958), 84-95.

Halley, R. A. "A Rebel Newspaper's War Story," *American Historical Magazine* 8 (January 1903), 1:124-149.

Hamilton, J.G. deRoulhac, "Lincoln and the South," *Sewanee Review* 17 (April 1909), 2:129-138.

Hardee, Charles Seton Henry. "Reminiscences of Charles Seton Henry Hardee," *Georgia Historical Quarterly* 12 (1928): 264-265.

Harwell, Richard Barksdale, "Confederate Anti-Lincoln Literature," *Lincoln Herald* 54 (Fall 1951): 3.

Huff, Lawrence. "Joseph Addison Turner, Southern Editor During the Civil War," *Journal of Southern History* 19 (November 1963): 468-485.

Inzer, John W. "How the News of the Assassination of President Lincoln was Received by Confederate Prisoners on Johnson's Island in April 1865," *Gulf States Historical Magazine* 1 (July 1902-Mayr 1903): 194-198.

Mallory, Stephen, "Last Days of the Confederate Government," *McClure's Magazine* 16 (1902): 242-243.

Owsley, Frank L. "A Southerner's View of Abraham Lincoln," *Georgia Review* 12 (Spring 1958), 1:5-17.

Park, Robert E. "Diary of Robert E. Park, Twelfth Alabama Regiment," *Southern Historical Papers* 3 (June 1877) 6:245-254.

_____ . "Propaganda in History," *Tyler's Quarterly Historical and Genealogical Magazine* 1 (April 1920) 4:223-224.

Reid, R. L. "Louisiana and Lincoln's Assassination: Reactions in a Southern State," *Southern Historian* 6 (Spring 1985) 22:20-27.

Rutledge, Archibald, "A Southerner Views Lincoln," *Scribner's Magazine* 83 (February 1928): 204-213.

_____ . "Lincoln, A Southern View. *The Reviewer* 5 (January 1925): 1.

_____ . "The South as it is by our Special Correspondent from Richmond on July 12, 1865," *Nation* 1 (1865): 110.

Steen, Ralph W. "Texas Newspapers and Lincoln," *Southern Historical Quarterly* 51 (January 1948) 3:199-212.

Talmadge, John E. "Savannah's Yankee Newspapers," *Georgia Review* 12 (Spring 1958): 66-72.

Turner, Joseph Addison, "Joseph Addison Turner: Southern Editor During the Civil War," Lawrence Huff, ed. *Journal of Southern History* 19 (November 1963).

Walmsley, James E. "The Last Meeting of the Confederate Cabinet," *Mississippi Valley Historical Review* 6 (1919-1920): 336-349.

Washington, Booker T. "Lincoln and the Black Man," *Alexander's Magazine* 7 (February 1909): 147-148.

Wight, Willard E., ed. "The Bishop of Natchez on the Death of Lincoln," *Lincoln Herald* 58 (Fall 1956): 13-14.

Wiley, Bell Irvin. "Billy Yank and Abraham Lincoln," *Abraham Lincoln Quarterly* 6 (June 1950) 2:104-119.

Yates, Richard E. "Governor Vance and the End of the War in North Carolina," *North Carolina Historical Review* 18 (October 1941): 4:315.

Published Memoirs, Biographies, Commentaries

Alfriend, Frank H. *The Life of Jefferson Davis*. Chicago: Claxton Publishing House, 1868.

Andrews, Eliza F. *The War Time Journal of a Georgia Girl, 1864-1865*. Edited by Spencer B. King, Jr. Macon, Ga.: Ardivan Press, 1960.

Burge, Dolly Sumner. *A Woman's Wartime Journal*. Macon, Ga.: J. W. Burke Co., 1927.

Campbell, John A. *Reminiscences and Documents Relating to the Civil War During the Year 1865*. Baltimore, 1887.

Chambers, William P. *My Journal*. Jackson, MS: Mississippi Historical Society, Vol 5, Centenary Series, 1925.

Chesnut, Mary Boykin. *A Diary From Dixie*. New York: Peter Smith Co., 1919.

_____. *Mary Chesnut's Civil War*. Edited by C. Vann Woodward. New Haven: Yale University Press, 1981.

Clopton, Virginia Clay. *A Belle of the Fifties: Memoirs of Mrs. [Virginia] Clay [Clopton] of Alabama, Covering Social and Political Life in*

Washington and the South, 1854-1866. Edited by Ada Sterling. London: Wm. Heinemenn, 1905.

Cumming, Katharine H. *A Northern Daughter and a Southern Wife: The Civil War Reminiscences and Letters of Katharine H. Cumming, 1860-1865*. Virginia: Richmond County Historical Society, 1976.

Cumming, Kate. *Kate: The Journal of a Confederate Nurse*. Edited by Richard Barksdale Harwell. Baton Rouge: Louisiana State University Press, 1959.

Davis, William C. *Breckinridge: Statesman, Soldier, Symbol*. Baton Rouge: Louisiana State University Press, 1974.

Flood, Charles Bracelen. *Lee: The Last Years*. Boston: Houghton-Mifflin Co., 1981.

Forrest, Douglas French, CSN. *Odyssey in Gray: A Diary of Confederate Service*. Edited by William N. Still, Jr. Richmond: The Virginia State Library, 1979.

Gordon, George H. *A War Diary of Events in the War of the Great Rebellion, 1863-1865*. Boston: James R. Osgood Co., 1882.

Govan, Gilbert G., and Livingston, James A. *A Different Valor: The Story of General Joseph E. Johnston, C.S.A.* Indianapolis, Indiana: Bobbs-Merrill, 1956.

Hardin, Lizzie. *The Private War of Lizzie Hardin*. Edited by G. Glenn Clift. Frankfort, Kentucky: The Kentucky Historical Society, 1965.

Heartsill, William Willison. *Fourteen Hundred and Ninety One Days in the Confederate Army*. Edited by Bell I. Wiley. 2nd Edition. Jackson, Tennessee: McCowart-Mercer Press, 1953.

Johnston, Richard Malcolm, and Brown, William Hand. *Life of Alexander H. Stephens*. Philadelphia, 1884.

Jones, John B. *A Rebel War Clerk's Diary*. Edited by Earl Schenck Miers. New York: A. S. Barnes & Co., 1961.

Koerner, Gustave, *Memoirs of Gustave Koerner*. 2 Vols. Edited by Thomas J. McCormack. Cedar Rapids, Iowa, 1890.

Lane, Mills, B., Ed. *William T. Sherman*. Savannah, Georgia: The Beehive Press, 1971.

LeConte, Emma. *When the World Ended: The Diary of Emma LaConte*. Edited by Earl Schenck Miers. New York: Oxford University Press, 1957.

Lunt, Dolly S. *A Woman's Wartime Journal*. New York: The Century Company, 1918.

Marcus, Jacob Rader. *Memoirs of American Jews, 1775-1865*. Vol. 3. Philadelphia: The Jewish Publishing Society of America, 1955.

Martin, Waldo E. Jr., *The Mind of Frederick Douglas*. Chapel Hill: University of North Carolina Press, 1984.

McDonald, Cornelia. *A Diary with Reminiscences of the War and Refugee Life In the Shenandoah Valley. 1860-1865*. Nashville, Tennessee: Cullen and Ghertner, 1934.

McGuire, Judith Brockenbrough. *Diary of a Southern Refugee*. New York: Doubleday, Page, 1968.

[McGuire, Dorothy Brockenbrough] *Diary of a Southern Refugee During the War by a Lady of Virginia*. New York: E. J. Hale & Son, 1868.

Mitchell, Betty L. *Edmund Ruffin: A Biography*. Bloomingdale: Indiana University Press, 1981.

Morgan, W. H. *Personal Reminiscences of the War of 1861-65*. Lynchburg, Virginia: J.P. Bell Co., 1911.

Nuermberger, Ruth Ketring. *The Clays of Alabama: A Planter-Lawyer-Politician Family*. Lexington: University of Kentucky Press, 1958.

Pearson, Elizabeth Ware, ed. *Letters from Port Royal Written at the Time of the Civil War*. Boston: W. B. Clark Co., 1906.

Ravenal, Henry William. *The Private Journal of Henry William Ravenal, 1958-1887*. Edited by Arney Robinson Childs. Columbia: University of South Carolina Press, 1947.

Ross, Ishbel. *First Lady of the South: The Life of Mrs. Jefferson Davis*. New York: Harper and Brothers, n.d.

Sherman, William T. *Memoirs*. Vol. 2. New York, 1875.

Smith, Daniel E. Huger; Smith, Alice R. Huger; and Childs, Arney R., eds. *Mason Smith Family Letters, 1860-1865*. Columbia: University of South Carolina Press, 1950.

Stephens, Alexander H. *Recollections of Alexander H. Stephens: His Diary Kept When a Prisoner at Fort Warren, Boston Harbor, 1865.* Edited by Myrta Lockett Avary. New York: Doubleday, Page & Co., 1910.

Strode, Hudson. *Jefferson Davis: Tragic Hero, the Last Twenty-Five Years, 1865-1889.* New York: Harcourt Brace, 1964.

Stone, Kate [Sarah Katherine Stone Holmes], *Brokenburn: The Journal of Kat Stone, 1861-1868.* Edited by John Q. Anderson. Baton Rouge: Louisiana State University Press, 1955.

Toney, Marcus B. *The Privations of a Private.* Nashville, Tennessee: Printed by the author, 1905.

Towne, Laura M. *Letters and Diary of Laura M. Towne, Written from the Sea Islands of South Carolina.* Edited by Rupert Sergent Holland. Cambridge: The Riverside Press, 1912.

Williams, Thomas Harry. *Pierre Gustave Toufant Beauregard: Napoleon in Gray.* Baton Rouge: Louisiana State University Press, 1954.

Books, Pamphlets, and Published Proceedings

Anderson, Galusha. *The Story of a Border City During the Civil War.* [St. Louis] Boston, Little Brown, 1908.

Andrews, J. Cutler. *The South Reports the Civil War.* Princeton, New Jersey: Princeton University Press, 1970.

The Assassination of A. Lincoln and the Attempted Assassination of Wm. H. Seward, Sec. of State, & Fred W. Seward, Asst. Sec. of State on the Evening of 14 Apr. 1865. Expressions of Condolence & Sympathy Inspired by These Events. Washington D.C.: Government Printing Office, 1867.

Avary, Myrta Lockett. *Dixie After the War.* New York: Doubleday Page, 1906.

Barrett, John G. *The Civil War in North Carolina.* Chapel Hill: The University of North Carolina Press, 1963.

Barr, Thomas Hughes. *A discourse delivered by T. H. Barr at Canaan Center April 19, 1865, on the Occasion of the Funeral Obsequies of our*

Late President, A. Lincoln. Wooster Ohio: Republican Steam Power Press, 1865. Emory University Microfilm Collection.

Basler, Roy P.; Marion Dolores Pratt; and Lloyd A. Dunlap, eds. *The Collected Works of Abraham Lincoln*. New Brunswick, New Jersey: Rutgers University Press, 1953-1955, 9 Vols.

Beecher, Henry Ward. *Oration at the Raising of the Old Flag at Sumter; and Sermon on the Death of Abraham Lincoln, President of the United States*. Manchester, England: E. A. Ireland Co., 1865.

Bill, Alfred Hoyt. *The Beleagued City: Richmond, 1861-1865*. New York: Knopf, 1956.

Bishop, Jim. *The Day Lincoln Was Shot*. New York: Harper and Brothers, 1955.

Blackwell, O. W. *Lincoln As the South Should Know Him*. Raleigh, N.C.: Manly's Battery Chapter, Children of the Confederacy, 1915.

Bode, Carl. *Maryland, A Bicentennial History*. New York: W. W. Norton, 1977.

Brantley, Rabun L. *Georgia Journalism of the Civil War Period*. Nashville: George Peabody College for Teachers, 1929.

Bryan, T. Conn. *Confederate Georgia*. Athens: University of Georgia Press, 1953.

Capers, Gerald M., Jr. *The Biography of a River Town: Memphis, Its Heroic Age*. Chapel Hill: University of North Carolina Press, 1939.

Capers, Gerald M. *Occupied City: New Orleans under the Federals, 1862-1865*. Lexington: University of Kentucky Press, 1965.

Carter, Hodding. *The Angry Scar: The Story of Reconstruction*. Garden City, New York: Doubleday, 1959.

Carter, Hodding. *Their Words Were Bullets: The Southern Press in War, Reconstruction, and Peace*. Athens: University of Georgia Press, 1969.

Cash, W. J. *The Mind of the South*. New York: Knopf, 1960.

Channing, Stephen A. *Kentucky: A History*. New York: W. W. Norton, 1977.

Clark, Thomas D. *The South Since Appomattox: A Century of Regional Change*. New York: Oxford University Press, 1967.

Coddington, David S. *Eulogy to Abraham Lincoln*, Delivered at Citadel Square, Charleston, S.C. on May 6, 1865 at the Request of the Officers and Soldiers in the Northern District, Department of the South. New York: Baker and Godwin, Printers, 1865.

Corley, Florence Fleming, *Confederate City: Augusta, Georgia*. Columbia: University of South Carolina Press, 1960.

Coulter, E. Merton. *The Civil War and Readjustment in Kentucky*. Chapel Hill: The University of North Carolina Press, 1926.

_____. *The South During Reconstruction, 1865-1877*. Baton Rouge: Louisiana State University Press, 1947.

Cox, LaWanda. *Lincoln and Black Freedom, A Study in Presidential Leadership*. Columbia: University of South Carolina Press, 1981.

Crabb, Alfred Leland. *Nashville: Personality of a City*. New York: Bobbs-Merrill Co., 1960.

Current, Richard N. *The Lincoln Nobody Knows*. New York: Hill and Wang, First American Century Series, 1963.

Currie, James T. *Enclave: Vicksburg and her Plantations, 1863-1870*. Jackson: University Press of Mississippi, 1980.

Dabney, Thomas Ewing. *One Hundred Great Years: The Story of the Times Picayune from Founding to 1940*. Baton Rouge: Louisiana State University Press, 1944.

Dabney, Virginius. *Richmond: The Story of a City*. Garden City, N.Y.: Doubleday & Co., 1976.

Davidson, J. W. *Resolutions Adopted at a Meeting of the Officers of the Army and Navy and Citizens of Natchez on the Death of the President of the United States. Natchez, Mississippi, 1865*. A printed copy is available at the Rare Book and Special Collections Division of the Library of Congress, Washington, D.C.

Davis, Jefferson. *The Rise and Fall of the Confederate Government*. New York, 1881.

Davis, Kenneth C. *Don't Know Much About the Civil War.* New York: William Morrow and Company, 1996.

Davis, Michael. *The Image of Lincoln in the South*. Knoxville: The University of Tennessee Press, 1971.

Davis, William C. *The Deep Waters of the Proud. The Imperiled Union, 1861-1865.* New York: Doubleday, 1982. Vol. 1.

Dawson, Sarah Morgan. *A Confederate Girl's Diary*, with Introduction by Warrington Dawson. Boston: Hougton Mifflin, 1913.

_____. Edited with a Foreword and Notes by James I. Robertson, Jr. Bloomington: Indiana State University Press, 1972.

Donald, David Herbert. *Lincoln.* New York: Simon and Schuster, 1996.

Durden, Robert F. *The Gray and the Black: The Confederate Debate on Emancipation.* Baton Rouge: Louisiana State University Press, 1972.

Fehrenbacher, Don E. *Prelude to Greatness: Lincoln in the 1850s.* Stanford, California: Stanford University Press, 1960.

_____. *The Changing Image of Lincoln in American Historiography.* Oxford: The Clarendon Press, 1968.

Fehrenbach, T. R. *Lone Star: A History of Texas and the Texans.* New York: Macmillan, 1968.

Foote, Shelby. *The Civil War: A Narrative, Fredericksburg to Meridian.* New York: Random House, 1963.

Fornell, Earl Wesley. *The Galveston Era.* Austin: University of Texas Press, 1961.

Glenn, William Wilkins. *Between North and South: A Maryland Journalist Views to the Civil War.* Edited by Bayley Ellen Marks and Mark Norton Schotz. Teaneck, New York: Fairleigh Dickinson University Press, 1976.

Govan, Gilbert E., and Ligingood, James W. *A Different Valor: The Story of General Joseph E. Johnston, C.S.A.* New York: Bobbs-Merrill, 1956.

Griffith, Louis Turner, and Talmadge, John Erwin. *Georgia Journalism 1763-1951.* Athens: University of Georgia Press, 1951.

Hanchett, William. *The Lincoln Murder Conspiracies.* Chicago: University of Illinois Press, 1983.

Hancock, Harold Bell. *Delaware During the Civil War: A Political History.* Wilmington: Historical Society of Delaware, 1961.

Hanna, A. J. *Flight into Oblivion*. Richmond: Johnson Publishing Co., 1938.

Hertzberg, Steven. *Strangers Within the Gate City: The Jews of Atlanta, 1845-1915*. Philadelphia: The Jewish Publication of Society of America, 1978.

Hesseltine, William Best. *The South in American History*. New York: Prentice-Hall, Inc., 1943.

Hoffecker, Carol E., *Delaware: A Bicentennial History*. New York: W. W. Norton, 1977.

Howell, J. B. *Special Collections in Libraries of the Southeast*. Published for the Southeastern Library Association. Jackson, Mississippi.: Howick House, 1978.

Hyman, Harold M., and Wiecek, William M. *Equal Justice Under the Law: Constitutional Development, 1835-1875*. New York: Harper & Row, 1982.

Hyman, Harold M. *Era of the Oath: Northern Loyalty Tests During the Civil War and Reconstruction*. Philadelphia: University of Pennsylvania Press, 1959.

_____. *Union and Confidence, the 1860s*. New York: Thomas Y. Crowell Co., 1976.

_____. "With Malice Toward Some: Scholarship (or Something Less) on the Lincoln Murder." Address delivered to the Abraham Lincoln Association, February, 1978. Springfield Illinois, c1979.

Jarmon, J. Wagner. *Abram [sic] Lincoln and South Carolina*. Philadelphia: D. E. Thompson, 1861.

Johns, John E. *Florida During the Civil War.* Gainesville: University of Florida Press, 1963.

Jones, Katherine M. *Heroines of Dixie*. New York: Bobbs-Merrill, 1955.

Kerby, Robert L. *Kirby Smith's Confederacy, The Trans-Mississippi South*. New York: Columbia University Press, 1972.

Korn, Bertran W. *American Jewry and the Civil War*. Cleveland, Ohio: World Publishing, 1951.

Lamont, D. S., ed. *War of the Rebellion. Official Records of the Union and Confederate Armies,* Series 1, Part 1. Washington, D.C.: Government Printing Office, 1895.

Litwack, Leon F. *Been in the Storm So Long: The Aftermath of Slavery*. New York: Alfred A. Knopf, 1979.

Long, E. B. *The Civil War Day by Day: An Almanac, 1861-1865*. Garden City, New York: Doubleday, 1971.

McCrary, Peyton. *Abraham Lincoln and Reconstruction: The Louisiana Experiment*. Princeton, NJ: Princeton University Press, 1978.

McDowell, Robert Emmett. *City of Conflict: Louisville in the Civil War, 1861-1865*. Louisville, KY: Louisville Civil War Round Table, 1962.

McIlwaine, Shields. *Memphis Down in Dixie*. New York: E. P. Dutton, 1948.

McPherson, James M. *The Negros' Civil War: How American Negros Felt and Acted During the Civil War*. New York: Pantheon Books, 1965.

Massey, Mary Elizabeth. *Bonnet Brigades*. Edited by Allan Nevins. New York: Alfred A. Knopf, 1966.

Mitgang, Herbert. *Abraham Lincoln: A Press Portrait*. Chicago: Quadrangle Books, 1971.

_____. *Lincoln as They Saw Him*. New York: Rhinehart, 1957.

Myers, Robert Manson, ed. *The Children of Pride*. New Haven: Yale University Press, 1971.

Neely, Mark E. *The Abraham Lincoln Encyclopedia*. New York: McGraw-Hill, 1982.

Nevins, Allan. *The Emergence of Lincoln, Douglas, Buchanan, and Party Chaos, 1857-1859*, Vol 1. New York: Charles Scribner's Sons. 1950.

Nicolay, John G. and Hay, John. *Abraham Lincoln: A History*. Edited by Paul M. Angle, 1890. 10 vols. Chicago: University of Chicago, 1966.

Oates, Stephen B. *Abraham Lincoln: The Man Behind the Myth*. New York: Harper & Row, 1984.

_____. *With Malice Toward None: The Life of Abraham Lincoln*. New York: Harper & Row, 1977.

Owen, Thomas McAdory. *History of Alabama and Dictionary of Alabama Biography.* Spartanburg, South Carolina: The Reprint Company, 1895.

Phillips, Ulrich B., ed. *The Correspondence of Robert Toombs, Alexander H. Stephens, and Howell Cobb.* New York: DaCapo Press, 1970.

Potter, David M. *The South and the Sectional Conflict.* Baton Rouge: Louisiana State University Press, 1968.

Quarles, Benjamin. *Lincoln and the Negro.* New York: Oxford University Press, 1962.

_____. *The Negro in the Civil War.* Boston: Little Brown & Co., 1953.

Randall, James G. *Lincoln and the South.* Baton Rouge: Louisiana State University Press, 1946.

_____, and Current, Richard N. *Lincoln the President: Last Full Measure.* New York: Dodd, Mead, 1955.

Reed, Wallace Putnam. *History of Atlanta, Georgia.* Syracuse, New York: D. Mason, 1889.

Rehrenbach, T. R. *Lone Star: A History of Texas and the Texans.* New York: Macmillan, 1968.

Reynolds, Donald E. *Editors Make War: Southern Newspapers in the Secession Crisis.* Nashville, Tennessee: Vanderbilt University Press, 1970.

Richardson, James D. *A Compilation of the Messages and Papers of the Confederacy, Including Diplomatic Correspondence, 1861-1865,* 10 Volumes. National Literature and Art c1897, Reprint, Nashville, 1906.

Richmond at War: Richmond City Council Minutes of the Council, 1861-65. University of North Carolina Press, 1966.

Roland, Charles P. *Louisiana Sugar Plantations During the American Civil War.* Leiden: E. J. Brill Publisher, 1959.

Rose, Willie Lee. *Rehearsal for Reconstruction: The Port Royal Experiment.* New York: Bobbs-Merrill, 1964.

Ross, Ishbel, *First Lady of the South: The Life of Mrs. Jefferson Davis.* New York: Harper, 1958.

Sandburg, Carl. *Abraham Lincoln: The War Years.* New York: Harcourt Brace, 1939.

Sass, Herbert Ravenel. *Outspoken: 150 Years of the [Charleston] News and Courier.* Columbia: University of South Carolina Press, 1953.

Searcher, Victor. *Lincoln Today: An Introduction to Modern Lincolniana.* New York: Thomas Yoseloff, 1965.

Shugg, Roger W. *Origins of Class Struggle in Louisiana.* Baton Rouge: Louisiana State University Press, 1939.

Smith, Page. *Trial by Fire: A People's History of the Civil War.* New York: McGraw-Hill, 1982.

Stephens, Elise Hopkins. *Historic Huntsville: A City of New Beginnings.* Woodbine Hills, California: Winson Publications, 1984.

Stern, Phillip vanDoren. *An End to Valor: The Last Days of the Civil War.* Boston: Houghton-Mifflin, 1958.

Turner, Thomas Reed. *Beware the People Weeping: Public Opinion and the Assassination of Abraham Lincoln.* Baton Rouge: Louisiana State University Press, 1982.

"Two Letters on the Event of April 14, 1865." Bulletin 47 of the Clements Library, University of Michigan, February 12, 1946.

Walker, Peter F. *Vicksburg: A People at War, 1860-1865.* Chapel Hill: University of North Carolina Press, 1965.

Warmoth, Henry Clay. *War Politics and Reconstruction.* New York: McMillan, 1930.

Wiley, Bell Irvin. *Southern Negroes, 1861-1865.* Baton Rouge: Louisiana State University Press, 1965.

Winters, John David. *The Civil War in Louisiana.* Baton Rouge: Louisiana State University Press, 1963.

Index

PRESIDENT LINCOLN'S FUNERAL I